ANALYZING THE ISSUES

CRITICAL PERSPECTIVES ON
MILLENNIALS

Edited by Bridey Heing

Enslow Publishing

101 W. 23rd Street
Suite 240
New York, NY 10011
USA

enslow.com

Published in 2018 by Enslow Publishing, LLC
101 W. 23rd Street, Suite 240, New York, NY 10011

Library of Congress Cataloging-in-Publication Data

Names: Heing, Bridey, editor.
Title: Critical perspectives on millennials / edited by Bridey Heing.
Description: New York : Enslow Publishing, [2018] | Series: Analyzing the issues | Audience: Grade 9 to 12. | Includes bibliographical references and index.
Identifiers: LCCN 2017001292 | ISBN 9780766084858 (library-bound)
Subjects: LCSH: Generation Y--Juvenile literature. | Youth--Social conditions--21st century--Juvenile literature. | Generations--Juvenile literature.
Classification: LCC HQ799.5 .C75 2018 | DDC 305.2--dc23
LC record available at https://lccn.loc.gov/2017001292

Printed in China

To Our Readers: We have done our best to make sure all website addresses in this book were active and appropriate when we went to press. However, the author and the publisher have no control over and assume no liability for the material available on those websites or on any websites they may link to. Any comments or suggestions can be sent by email to customerservice@enslow.com.

Excerpts and articles have been reproduced with the permission of the copyright holders.

Photo Credits: Cover, alvarez/E+/Getty Images (people on computers), Thaiview/Shutterstock.com (background, pp. 4–5 background), gbreezy/Shutterstock.com (magnifying glass on spine); p. 4 Ghornstern/Shutterstock.com (header design element, chapter start background throughout book).

CONTENTS

INTRODUCTION

Millennials are a generation that has been discussed at length by everyone from marketing professionals to academic researchers. With much to set them apart from past generations, such as generation X or the baby boomers, millennials are a complex group of people coming into their own as a powerful force to be reckoned with. But who are the millennials, and what does it mean to categorize or attempt to understand an entire generation of people?

The term *millennial* refers to those born between roughly 1980 and 2000, although the exact range is debated by researchers. According to the Pew Research Center, millennials were born between 1981 and 1996, which means there is an estimated 75.3 million millennials in the United States. This makes them the largest living generation, edging out baby boomers (those born between 1946 and 1964) by about 400,000. The millennial generation is also growing thanks to immigration, with Pew estimating that by 2036 there will be 81.1 million millennials in the United States.[1]

Millennials grew up during a time of immense change, which means there are many differences between members of this generation. The oldest millennials were already in college before the internet became a common feature of everyday life, while the youngest millennials can't remember a time without it. The digital age has shaped our culture quickly. Millennials are the first generation of digital natives and who are able to recall what life was like before the internet. Events like the fall of the Berlin Wall in 1989, the dissolution of the Soviet Union in 1991, and the September 11 attacks reshaped the world as the millennials were growing up, and many millennials were entering college or the workforce when the 2008 financial crisis threatened the global economy. All of these factors make millennials a unique generation, faced with challenges and given advantages that the generations that came before struggle to fully comprehend.

This lack of comprehension can be seen in how millennials are discussed by researchers, the media, and average citizens. Often painted as lazy or entitled, millennials have been given a bad rap by many—sometimes even those in their own generation. But this doesn't take into account the research that shows millennials to be hardworking, innovative, and often times struggling with economic uncertainty. Nearly half of all millennials have student debt according to a study by Harvard University, and studies have found that the average student debt burden on millennials is around $40,000.[2] At the same time, job gains since the recession have not benefited millennials, who have lower incomes and less job mobility than past generations. Millennials are believed to be the first generation in United States history that won't do better economically than their parents, due in part to having to play catch-up because of debt and low wages.

But millennials also have a lot of advantages. They are resourceful and well educated—in fact, they are the most educated generation in US history. Millennials are changing the traditional career path in order to make it work for them, largely by embracing multiple jobs and casual work in what has become known as the "gig economy." They also care about social justice issues and are more socially liberal than past generations, with Pew finding that 57 percent of millennials see themselves as such.[3]

In this book, we'll look at research, opinion pieces, political speeches, and polls to get a sense of how millennials are shaping the world they live in and how the world sees them. We'll hear from presidents, business leaders, advocates, and journalists, all of whom have a unique take on what makes millennials who they are and what that means for the future. We'll also be asking questions about what we read, to help you decide for yourself what the United States's largest generation has to offer and overcome.

CHAPTER 1

WHO ARE THE MILLENNIALS?

As a generation, millennials are diverse and educated, meaning that it is difficult to pigeonhole the millions of individuals who make up this particular age group. Many have expressed concern that millennials are entitled or lazy, while others see the generation as hardworking and determined. While the truth is likely more complicated than either of those two stark characterizations, millennials are struggling to make their way. In the following pieces, authors look at the world millennials grew up in, how they were shaped by their collective experiences, and some of the criticism of the generation. Based on research and personal experience, each author offers a unique take on what defines the millennial generation.

"THE MYTH OF MILLENNIAL ENTITLEMENT WAS CREATED TO HIDE THEIR PARENTS' MISTAKES," BY SARAH KENDZIOR, FROM *QUARTZ*, JUNE 30, 2016

Three years ago, TIME magazine published a cover story called "The Me Me Me Generation—Millennials are lazy, entitled narcissists who still live with their parents." It was the print version of clickbait, designed to be devoured by TIME's Baby Boomer base, or perhaps flipped through angrily by millennials killing time at TIME's most reliable subscriber, the doctor's office. That is, if the millennials in question were lucky enough to have health insurance, which roughly 23% did not at the time.

Of course, these kinds of inconvenient statistics did not make it into the piece. When TIME's cover story was published, millennials were in the fourth year of the "jobless recovery," facing high unemployment, mounting debt, and an eroded social safety net. And yet, with breathtaking cluelessness, TIME framed the millennials' desperate search for stable work as a privileged character flaw—look at the kids too flaky to handle "choosing from a huge array of career options." The idea that today's young people are narcissistic and lazy lingers just beneath the surface.

Fast forward to 2016, and millennials are now valued as an electoral prize and a revenue source. Media coverage has adjusted accordingly. But the idea that today's young people are narcissistic and lazy lingers just beneath the surface. Browsing through news articles, two parallel worlds of millennials emerge. The first is inhabited by overtly political youth advocating for controversial initiatives like campus safe spaces. The second is filled with young consumers who are happy and prosperous yet prefer style over stuff—which, upon closer examination, is a euphemistic way of saying they cannot afford to buy much stuff anyway.

These narratives are more nuanced than TIME's ridiculous 2013 attempt to capture millennials, but they still fail to accurately portray the reality of young people's lives. For one thing, most depictions fail to define the age bracket of the cohort and relate it to historical context. In this way, critics often end up repackaging millennials' economic desperation as lifestyle choices, leading to a sort of generational gaslighting over what life in the new economy is really like.

Meanwhile, the shared experience of Americans who struggled as young adults in the aftermath of the Great Recession is played down in favor of trend pieces on the affectations of privileged youth or the phenomenon of "side hustles." Critics often end up repackaging millennials' economic desperation as lifestyle choices. Analysts puzzle over why young Americans forgo things like banks and marriage and houses, and come up with answers like "preference for urban locations with lots of entertainment and lifestyle choices."

Indeed, terms like "preference" and "choice" still dominate media coverage of millennials. But if anything holds this tenuously defined generation together, it is a lack of options. Americans who have lived much of their adult lives in the aftermath of the Great Recession have lower incomes, less mobility, and greater financial dependence on older relatives than any other generation in modern history. Many millennials do not have a lot of choice. They are merely reacting to lost opportunity.

Part of the confusion lies in the way we define generations in the US, a series of labels that are as unclear as they are inconsistent. Let's start with a bit of history. "Generation X," the generation that predates millennials, is a term coined by Douglas Coupland (born in 1961) to define people born in the 1960s and early 1970s. Gen Xers were young adults in 1990 when Coupland's book, *Generation X: Tales for an Accelerated Culture*, was published. Bizarrely, Americans who were children at the time of Coupland's publication have now been assimilated into his generational cohort. Generation X has been redefined as Americans born roughly between the mid-1960s and the mid-1980s.

"Millennials" have writers William Strauss and Neil Howe to thank for the label. This generation has also been defined inconsistently, with dates ranging between the late 1970s and 2000. The overlap between Gen X and millennials is a source of frustration for the overlapping group of Americans born between the late 1970s and the early 1980s, who have named themselves, in honor of their neglected relevance, things like "The Oregon Trail Generation" and "Generation Catalano." The influential Pew Research Center draws the line at 1981, however, a standard that is most often applied by media outlets.

Nevertheless, there's a good case to be made that even Pew's generational labels should be abandoned. In a brilliant piece posted on Medium, "F*** You, I'm not a Millennial", Patrick Hipp makes the case for the return of the term "Gen Y," once used to define those born between 1976-1990 who grew up "in tandem with the internet" and experienced the birth of digital culture as the institutions they grew up with crumbled around them.

Hipp's generational breakdown makes sense because it defines generations in fourteen-year increments shaped by the ages of its cohorts at times of sweeping change, such as the advent of the internet or the terror attacks of 9/11. This model emphasizes how historical circumstances shape behavior and expectations—a nuance not present in sloppy coverage by the media. In 2014, *The New York Times* published a piece on a 37-year-old "millennial," prompting *Slate* writer Amanda Hess to posit that "millennial" was *Times* code for "a few rich white people in New York doing something." This theory seemed born out in fact in 2016, when Andrew Boryga's *Fusion* piece on low-income youth of color noted that many had never even heard the word "millennial," much less related to its popular characterization.

With all the confusion over and misrepresentations of younger generations, is it worth trying to define them at all? If recent events are any indication, the answer is yes—if defined correctly.

In the UK, an elderly generation of Brits have voted against the wishes of a majority of the country's young people—most of whom voted to remain in the European Union. The inability of older generations to see how the economy has been fundamentally restructured since the Great Recession leads to short-sighted policies that young people, not boomers, will have to live with in the long run.

In the US election, the winner will help determine policies for workers far younger than either Baby Boomer candidate. he eventual winner will help determine policies for American workers far younger than the candidates. Let's hope that these policies are shaped by what young

Americans' lives are actually like, not by what older elites see on stereotypically "millennial" shows like Lena Dunham's HBO hit "Girls" or read in trend pieces focusing on the idiosyncrasies of affluent youth.

For most Americans under 40, life since 2008 has been a struggle to survive. But it is worth noting that plenty of older Americans share the same struggles as their younger peers. Many older people laid off in the recession were unable to regain good jobs. There are plenty of older people with few retirement savings, with their finances drained from paying for both elderly parents and jobless children. We need to acknowledge the way our struggles are intertwined, instead of allowing the media to stoke manufactured class and generational resentment.

"Millennials" have become both a media scapegoat for, and a distraction from, widespread economic suffering. Having experienced no economy other than the recession's false recovery, young Americans have arguably suffered the most. The remedy lies not in judging their lifestyle choices—or worse yet, perpetuating the illusion that they have money to burn—but by acknowledging the new economy for what it is: a structural crisis, one that future generations will share. Millennials keep getting older, but their problems stay the same age.

1. What are some of the issues and problems that millennials face?

2. Why would previous generations consider millennials "lazy" or "entitled"?

"IN DEFENSE OF MILLENNIALS," BY GABRIELLE LEWINE, FROM *PSYCHOLOGY TODAY*, JUNE 8, 2016

Let's play a game. When I say the word "millennial", what's the first word that comes to mind? Perhaps some version of "lazy, entitled narcissists," per Joel Stein's controversial *Time* article about the "me, me, me generation." Or maybe you're more of a 60 Minutes type, and CBS correspondent Morley Safer's "narcissistic praise hounds" fit the bill. Take a moment to search for images of "millennials" on Google, and you'll be met with pages and pages of these fabled creatures staring at screens, taking selfies, or staring at screens in order to take selfies. It's safe to say that millennials get a bad rap.

What is a millennial, you ask? The millennials make up the generation born between 1980 and the late 1990s. This means the second wave of millennials are currently between the ages of 18-26, smack in the middle of a period of life termed "emerging adulthood" by developmental psychologist Jeffrey Arnett. Psychologists have defined emerging adulthood as a unique period during which young adults have the chance to explore possibilities in the domains of love, work, and worldview, before adult responsibilities such as marriage and parenthood descend on them. This concept has been used to understand the delayed age of marriage (for women: from a median of 21 in 1970 to a median of 26 in 2010), the delayed age of first childbirth (from an average of 21 in 1970 to an average of 26 in 2014), and the increasing rate of pursuing further education after high school (from 14% in 1940 to >60% in the mid-90s). This is fitting, as emerging adulthood has its own unique set of developmental tasks, or benchmarks that indicate one's success during a particular life stage. According to this theory, finding a career is one of the key tasks of emerging adulthood.

Millennials are entering the workforce in staggering numbers, and will represent over half of working adults by 2020. As this reality draws closer, Baby Boomers and Gen X-ers in management positions are starting to panic. How are they supposed to manage these selfie-taking yoga-loving brats?! This excerpt from Morley Safer's aforementioned piece on millennials (forebodingly titled "The Millennials are Coming") sums up this sentiment best:

"They were raised by doting parents who told them they are special, played in little leagues with no winners or losers, or all winners. They are laden with trophies just for participating and they think your business-as-usual ethic is for the birds. ... They multi-task, talk, walk, listen, type, and text. And their priorities are simple: they come first."

Inflammatory editorials are one thing – scientific research is another. With the massive influx of millennials in the workplace, huge companies are hiring researchers and consultants to answer the question of how best to manage this generation. So, keeping in mind this generation of emerging adults diligently pursuing their developmental task of choosing a career, let's look at the science behind four common stereotypes about millennial workers: namely, that they are disloyal, needy, entitled, and casual.

The label of "disloyalty" comes from millennials' frequent job-hopping, which is backed up by statistics. Approximately 60% of millennials report having already changed jobs at least once in their young careers.

The average tenure of a millennial employee is 2 years (compared to 5 years for Gen X-ers and 7 years for Baby Boomers). This is a stark contrast from the employment model that these older generations met upon entering the workforce, the crux of which has been called the "psychological contract" between employers and employees. This psychological contract is an individual's perceptions about what mutual obligations exist in employer-employee relations, and for previous generations, it went something like: "We will hire you and treat you well, you will respond with hard work and loyalty to our organization."

Cue the 2007 recession. Early millennials saw this psychological contract broken as older employees were laid off in droves while higher performance was demanded of new employees and compensation flatlined. Never mind the many recent college graduates who, instead of finding the employment they sought, found an exponentially increasing interest rate on their college loan debt. Millennials have lower expectations for job security than the two generations before them, and it's no wonder! Why work for a system that's not working for you? While the same behavior 30 years ago may have been "disloyal", millennials' nomadic career journeys are to be expected: they adapted to the job market they entered.

"Neediness," when used to describe millennials in the workplace, usually refers to a higher need for feedback and monitoring than existing management is used to. How much feedback? Researchers have estimated that millennials need feedback from their supervisors at least once per month, which represents a shift from a workplace model where requiring less oversight indicates that you are doing a good job.

Organizational psychologists have suggested that this increased need for feedback may be a product of 2001's No Child Left Behind Act. With the shift in focus from process to outcome as a direct result of this legislation, the classroom environment also shifted such that feedback was constantly provided in order to assess progress toward standardized outcomes. The pejorative label of "needy" may come from managers who resent the extra work required to provide this teacher-like level of feedback. However, research has consistently shown that frequent and specific feedback helps to optimize performance. Therefore, not only is this so-called "neediness" an expected byproduct of millennials' educational environments, it also aligns with scientific research on best practice in management.

Now, for the real zinger, "entitled." Entitled is probably the first word many people associate with this generation: a Google search for "millennials are" has "entitled" among the top three suggested words to complete the search. Entitlement, in this context, essentially means expecting something for nothing. So, how well does this describe millennials in the workplace? Well, a global survey from 2014 conducted with 10,000 respondents indicated that 47% of millennials report working longer hours in the past 5 years, compared to 38% of Gen X-ers and 28% for Baby Boomers. Huh? That's right – millennials are working even longer hours compared to prior generations.

Okay, so Morley Safer's assertion that millennials want to "roll into work with their iPods and flip flops at noon, but still be CEO by Friday" doesn't check out with the fact that this generation is working harder and longer than ever. But there may be some truth behind the second half of his quote. Millennials, as a group, are more ambitious and more likely to actively seek career advancement, according to a study of motivational differences among generations. And their ambition is paying off: in a 2014 survey, 30% of millennials reported already holding management positions. Furthermore, researchers have pointed out that millennials were raised in the age of helicopter parenting, when overscheduling, micromanaging, high expectations and even higher pressure to succeed was the norm. The ambitious, progress-oriented emphasis that they bring to the workplace can be seen as a direct continuation of this emphasis during their school years.

And finally, millennials in the workplace are bemoaned for being too "casual." This applies not only to their well-documented desire for less formal work attire, but more generally to a push toward working remotely rather than working from an office. The discussion of work-from-home policies is intricately tied to technological developments that define the modern workplace. When office culture was first established, it was necessary to come to work in order to do your work. This is no longer the case. As some organizational psychologists say, "work is no longer a place you go, but a thing you do". And indeed, millennials do value work-life balance more than other generations, and rate it as an important contributor to overall job satisfaction.

Advocates of traditional 9-5 office work may dismiss demands for flexible work-from-home policies as just another example of lazy entitlement. But once again, these demands reflect a real cultural shift in work, family, and work-life balance as the millennial generation reaches adulthood. For example, millennials are almost twice as likely (78%) to have a partner that also works full time, compared to Baby Boomers (48%). Where family is concerned, the norm of working in an office reflected the reality of single-earner families, where one spouse went to work while the other stayed home for childcare purposes. Clearly, this is no longer typical, and rigid policies that don't allow working from home do not respond to the now-normative situation of dual-earner families with young children. These policies have been historically unfriendly to women, who have ended up sacrificing their careers or exiting the workforce in order to care for children. Demands for flexibility regarding working from home not only reflect the millennial generation's desire for more family-friendly workplace policies, but also come with a host of other benefits regarding productivity, employee morale, and the like.

A slew of disgruntled managers and clickbait journalists have generated the impression in popular media that millennials are disloyal, needy, entitled, and casual workers. Moment of truth: does this depiction stand up to research? No. Every generation entering the workforce has changed its structure and mores to reflect the realities of the time, and millennials are no different. Each of these derogatory labels hides a story of millennials adapting to a harsh job market, seamlessly incorporating technology into their work, and advocating for work policies that are family-friendly. Furthermore, these demands largely reflect what research supports: for example, the value of frequent feedback and the motivational power of work-from-home policies. Joel Stein, the author of the "me, me, me generation" *Time* article, began by saying "I am about to do what old people have done throughout history: call those younger than me lazy, entitled, selfish, and shallow." He's right – the pattern of older generations preferring to think their way of doing things is preferable to new ways they don't understand is timeless. The realities of the ways that millennials are changing the workforce reflect the more forgiving conclusion of Stein's article: "They're not a new species; they've just mutated to adapt to their environment."

1. Does the author see millennials as far different from previous generations? How are they the same or different, according to the author?

2. How did the recession impact the way millennials think about work and careers?

"THE MILLENNIAL MUDDLE," BY ERIC HOOVER, FROM *THE CHRONICLE OF HIGHER EDUCATION*, OCTOBER 11, 2009

Kids these days. Just look at them. They've got those headphones in their ears and a gadget in every hand. They speak in tongues and text in code. They wear flip-flops everywhere. Does anyone really understand them?

Only some people do, or so it seems. They are experts who have earned advanced degrees, dissected data, and published books. If the minds of college students are a maze, these specialists sell maps.

Ask them to explain today's teenagers and twenty-somethings. Invite them to your campus to describe this generation's traits. Just make sure that they don't all show up at the same time. They would argue, contradict one another, and leave you more baffled than ever.

Figuring out young people has always been a chore, but today it's also an industry. Colleges and corporations pay experts big bucks to help them understand the fresh-faced hordes that pack the nation's dorms and office buildings. As in any business, there's variety as well as competition. One speaker will describe youngsters as the brightest bunch of do-gooders in modern history. Another will call them self-involved knuckleheads. Depending on the prediction, this generation either will save the planet, one soup kitchen at a time, or crash-land on a lonely moon where nobody ever reads.

Everyone in higher education has pondered "the Millennials," people born between 1982 and 2004 or there-abouts (the years themselves are a subject of debate). Ever since the term went prime time about a decade ago, a zillion words have been written about who Millennials are, how they think, and why they always _____. In short, Millennials talk is contagious.

Those who have shaped the nation's understanding of young people are not nearly as famous as their subjects, however. That's a shame, for these experts are colorful characters in their own right. Some are scholars, and some aren't. Many can recall watching the Beatles on a black-and-white television, and some grew up just before Barney the purple dinosaur arrived. Most can entertain an audience, though a few prefer to comb through statistics.

In other words, they're all different. But just for fun, let's stereotype them as smart, successful, and full of unshakeable opinions. Although they have described one another's work as "wrong," "unempirical," and "wildly mistaken," these experts have something in common: They are products of their time. In an era when the wants of young consumers have become a fixation for colleges and businesses alike, these unlikely entrepreneurs have fed a world with a bottomless craving for labels.

For as long as human hair has turned gray, elders have looked at their successors and frowned. "Children nowadays are tyrants," goes an old quotation widely attributed to Socrates. "They contradict their parents, chatter before company, gobble their food, and tyrannize their teachers." In 1855 a professor at Davidson College described college students as "indulged, petted, and uncontrolled at home ... with an undisciplined mind, and an uncultivated heart, yet with exalted ideas of personal dignity, and a scowling contempt for lawful authority." Albert Einstein opined that while classrooms are many, "the number of young people who genuinely thirst after truth and justice is small."

Criticizing the young is inevitable, but so, too, is change. In 2000, Neil Howe and William Strauss published *Millennials Rising: The Next Great Generation*, which cast turn-of-the-century teenagers as rule followers who were engaged, optimistic, and downright pleasant. The authors assigned them seven "core traits": special, sheltered, confident, team-oriented, conventional, pressured, and achieving. These conclusions were based on a hodge-podge of anecdotes, statistics, and pop-culture references, as well as on surveys of teachers and about 600 high-school seniors in Fairfax County, Va., which in 2007 became the first county in the nation to have a median household income of more than $100,000, about twice the national average.

The authors made a sweeping prediction. "This generation is going to rebel by behaving not worse, but better," they wrote of Millennials, a term they had coined. "Their life mission will not be to tear down old institutions that don't work, but to build up new ones that do." Such thinking promised to give educators, not to mention tens of millions of parents, a warm feeling. Who wouldn't want to hear that their kids are special?

Mr. Howe and Mr. Strauss were unlikely messengers of this "good-news revolution." After all, they were not social scientists; they were Washington wonks. At the time, Mr. Howe was an economic-policy consultant and an adviser to the Concord Coalition, a nonpartisan group that supports deficit reduction and Social Security. Mr. Strauss, who had worked in President Ford's White House and as a staffer in the U.S. Senate, was the director of the Capitol Steps, a satirical singing group. The two shared political views, Ivy League degrees, and a love of history.

The latter had inspired them to write their first book, *Generations: The History of America's Future, 1584 to 2069*. Although *Millennials Rising* would fill the bookshelves of college presidents, deans, and professors, *Generations* laid the foundation for the authors' writings on students. Published in 1991, the elaborate chronicle contained a bold, almost mystical theory: that the nation's entire history had revolved in a predictable cycle of spiritual awakenings and secular crises. In turn, each generation fit one of four distinct archetypes (prophet, nomad, hero, and artist), which have repeated continuously in the same sequence. As surely as autumn follows summer, the Millennials would become the next "hero" generation, destined for coming-of-age triumphs, intent on taking action and building community, just like the "G.I. Generation" decades before.

This retelling of history impressed many reviewers, as well as some influential people. Former Vice President Al Gore—who graduated from Harvard University with Mr. Strauss—called *Generations* the most stimulating book on American history he'd ever read. He even sent a copy to each member of Congress. Yet *Publishers Weekly* called the book "as woolly as a newspaper horoscope." And in academe, scholars chuckled. Nothing like this had ever been written with a straight face.

Arthur E. Levine, a former president of the Teachers College of Columbia University and co-author of *When Hope and Fear Collide: A Portrait of Today's College Student*, remains unimpressed. "Generational images are stereotypes," says Mr. Levine, now president of the Woodrow Wilson Foundation. "There are some differences that stand out, but there are more similarities between students of the past and the present. But if you wrote a book saying that, how interesting would that book be?"

Generations established its creators as pioneers in a burgeoning field. They soon became media darlings, best-selling authors, and busy speakers. *Generations* would popularize the idea that people in a particular age group share distinct personae and values by virtue of occupying the same "place" in time as they grow up. In turn, this would affirm the notion that Millennials were a riddle waiting to be solved.

These days people all over the world seek Mr. Howe's advice about Millennials. Mellow and soft-spoken, he listens for rhythms in history. Meandering through a conversation, he can relate the generational significance of the

RMS *Lusitania* to that of F. Scott Fitzgerald, *Animal House's* Bluto Blutarsky, and Louisiana's Bobby Jindal, the first U.S. governor of Indian descent—all in five minutes. Close your eyes, and Mr. Howe, 57, might be a philosophical ex-hippie, riffing on how the universe fits together.

In fact, he's a well-connected consultant who runs a bustling business, LifeCourse Associates, from the ground floor of his spacious home in Great Falls, Va., just outside Washington. Mr. Strauss died of cancer in 2007, and Mr. Howe now works side by side with three employees, the oldest of whom is 28. Soon the company plans to publish *Millennials in the Workplace*, which follows several other books, such as *Millennials Go to College, Millennials & K-12 Schools*, and *Millennials and the Pop Culture*.

On a recent Monday afternoon, Mr. Howe's telephone is ringing. Evidence of several half-finished projects covers his desk. Soon he must submit a draft of an article about changing moods throughout American history, which the *Harvard Business Review* plans to publish. He must prepare for several trips, including a visit to the United Nations, where he will discuss "global aging and demographic security." On his computer screen are rainbows of charts, on crime, drinking habits, and pregnancy rates among young people.

A deliveryman arrives with packages. "The market is so vast," Mr. Howe says. "There are so many projects that I don't have time to do." As if to prove this, he tells his colleagues that he's thinking of canceling a contract with a client—a state chapter of the National Guard—that's haggling over some small details. "They're all bureaucrats!" he says.

Each year Mr. Howe gives about 60 speeches, often followed by customized workshops. He speaks at colleges, elementary schools, and corporations, and he charges between $5,000 and $14,000, plus travel expenses. He has consulted with various colleges, including Arizona State University, Dartmouth College, Georgetown University, and the University of Texas. His recommendations have influenced the mailings admissions offices send, the extracurricular activities colleges offer, the way professors teach, and even the food students eat. LifeCourse Associates has a partnership with Chartwells, a food-service company that has redefined campus cafeterias and menus at many colleges (think small-group seating and made-to-order meals).

Mr. Howe has also consulted with some of the globe's biggest companies, including Nike, Hewlett-Packard, and Kraft Nabisco. Recently an investment firm in Prague hired him to do a demographic forecast. Soon the U.S. Army's lucrative advertising contract will go up for grabs, and Mr. Howe is advising an agency that will compete for it.

A while back, the Ford Motor Company hired him to answer a question: What kind of car would Millennials want to buy? He advised the company to consider the power of "hero myths"—Hercules, Superman, and the boys of Iwo Jima—in its marketing. "Millennials want to do big things," he wrote in a report for Ford. "Even when driving back and forth to community college in a Focus … their future will be anything but mundane."

Those are the grand terms in which Mr. Howe thinks, even when he's just sitting here, shooting the breeze, with his brown walking shoes propped on a desk. When this thirtysomething reporter makes an offhand observation, he remarks, "That's such an Xer thing to say." He means

Generation X, whose members hail from 1961 to 1981, according to his timeline. Because they tend to be skeptical, hardened pragmatists, he says, they have trouble seeing what's so great about today's kids. For emphasis, he pauses, then says of Millennials, "They are so special."

And who is Mr. Howe? "A typical boomer," he says. There is such a thing, he insists. That historical events shape people of a given generation in specific ways is a pillar of his philosophy. The Vietnam War was one event that shaped him. As a student at the University of California at San Diego, he watched a national debate boil. In 1970, when he was a freshman, a fellow student named George Winne Jr. set himself ablaze on the campus while protesting the war and died the next day. Mr. Howe later transferred to Berkeley, where tie-dyed curtains hung in fraternity windows and students bagged classes to hold teach-ins. Everywhere, he saw a cultural rift between young and old. "There was a hysteria in the air," he says. "A sense that we were headed for the apocalypse."

A similar feeling swept the nation in September 2001, just as the first Millennials were settling into college campuses. The day after the terrorist attacks on New York and the Pentagon, Mr. Howe appeared on CNN to discuss historical cycles, a subject he and Mr. Strauss had described in a 1997 book called *The Fourth Turning*, which described four repeating "saecula," or seasons, of history—awakenings, unravelings, crises, and highs. Did the smoldering twin towers portend a crisis era? The day after the interview, *The Fourth Turning* appeared in Amazon's top 20.

Weeks later, Mr. Howe and Mr. Strauss flew to San Antonio to give a keynote speech at the National

Association for College Admission Counseling's annual conference. Attendees stood and sang "God Bless America." In the convention center, as on college campuses and town squares, people perceived that a line had just been drawn in the sand of history. Soon *Newsweek* published a cover story called "Generation 9-11," which described the unprecedented attacks as a "defining moment" for high-school and college students.

The aftermath made many people more receptive to the message of *Millennials Rising*, Mr. Howe believes. "Whenever there's a change in social mood," he says, "it makes thinking about generations clearer."

As cheery as a bouquet of roses, the good news about Millennials intrigued many people who recruit, serve, and teach college students. Administrators and professors had long stereotyped the students walking through the campus gates, but as the 21st century began, higher education was evolving in ways that made the time ripe for a new and tidy explanation of contemporary undergraduates.

For one, colleges turned to marketing as never before. Among selective colleges, the decade brought intense competition for applicants. Even among less-selective institutions, recruitment meant expanding into new territories and reaching out to more-diverse students. Early-acceptance programs ballooned. Parents morphed into co-purchasers. Deans embraced holistic evaluations, attempting to peer deeper into hearts and noggins. Sophisticated statistical models predicted who would enroll—and at what price.

Meanwhile, technology changed the application process. The Web was the Wild West of the enrollment profession, and with it came "stealth applicants" and much uncertainty. Many admissions officials found themselves under pressure to meet ambitious enrollment goals while protecting the bottom line. Understanding the whys of students' attitudes and behaviors was more crucial than ever.

Amid this complexity, the Millennials message was not only comforting but empowering. "It tickled our ears," says Palmer H. Muntz, director of admissions and an enrollment-management consultant at Lincoln Christian University, in Illinois. "It packaged today's youth in a way that we really wanted to see them. It gave us a formula for understanding them."

Over time, however, Mr. Muntz started to doubt the formula. Each year he visited many rural and urban high schools. He did not meet many students who had sweated their grades or taken standardized tests multiple times. *Millennials Go to College*, published in 2003, described an "intense new emphasis on preparation and planning" among students who were competing in a college-application "arms race," who thought about their futures in "five- or 10-year time horizons," and who perceived the high achievements of their peers as "a constant source of personal pressure."

Yet Mr. Muntz met few students who seemed to have these "pressured" and "achieving" traits. Generally, he saw what he had always seen—sharp kids, average kids, and kids with weaknesses, all with hopes and worries, floating day to day through teenage life. He wondered if the sample of students in *Millennials Rising* had corrupted the findings. After all, most students do not apply to top-20 colleges.

And so Mr. Muntz confronted a fact: To accept generational thinking, one must find a way to swallow two large assumptions. That tens of millions of people, born over about 20 years, are fundamentally different from people of other age groups—*and* that those tens of millions of people are similar to each other in meaningful ways. This idea is the underpinning of Mr. Howe's conclusion that each generation turns a historical corner, breaking sharply with the previous generation's traits and values.

Several researchers have blasted this theory of "nonlinear" social change. Some cite data from the Cooperative Institutional Research Program at the University of California at Los Angeles, which has conducted an annual survey of college freshmen since 1966. The survey, which provides a longitudinal view of trends, suggests that many changes among students happen gradually, not abruptly.

Moreover, the survey complicates the Millennials theory in numerous ways. According a recent report by the program, "American Freshmen: Forty Year Trends," today's students are not significantly busier, more confident, or more positive than they were in recent decades. Though more say they want to contribute to society, more also cite "being well off financially" as a goal. They are only slightly less likely to say they want to go to college to get a job, make money, or go to graduate school. They are not any more or less cooperative or competitive, nor do they seem more interested in developing a meaningful philosophy of life

Not long ago, Mr. Muntz attended a presentation about those findings. He has since decided to stop thinking in generational terms. "You can't just take one stamp and

CRITICAL PERSPECTIVES ON MILLENNIALS

at the University of Michigan at Ann Arbor, she discovered questionnaires that academic psychologists had designed to measure personality traits and attitudes. The questionnaires had been used widely since the 1950s, and most had been completed by college students and schoolchildren. That allowed her to compare changes in young people over time.

Like Mr. Howe and Mr. Strauss, Ms. Twenge concluded that when people were born shapes them more than (or at least as much as) where they were born or who their parents were. Yet she did not buy the idea that changes in students came suddenly. "Changes are linear; they happen over time," she says.

In *Millennials Rising*, Ms. Twenge did not find sufficient evidence to compare this generation with previous ones. Moreover, her findings did not come with a big smiley face. In 2006, Ms. Twenge described her research in her first book, *Generation Me: Why Today's Young Americans Are More Confident, Assertive, Entitled—and More Miserable Than Ever Before*. "I see no evidence that today's young people feel much attachment to duty or to group cohesion." Ms. Twenge wrote. "Young people have been consistently taught to put their own needs first and to focus on feeling good about themselves."

Ms. Twenge defined Generation Me as anyone born in the 1970s through the 1990s. Born in 1971, the author thus included herself in this generation. Many children of this era, she wrote, had been raised in a culture of constant praise, in which everyone got trophies and parents filled their children's ears with assurances that they were unique, talented, and special. Call it too much of a good thing. Among other outcomes, she found, the "self-esteem movement" had led to a rise in narcissism. She had analyzed some 15,000 students' responses to a questionnaire called the Narcissistic Personality Inventory between 1987 and 2006. The inventory contained statements like, "I think I am a special person," "I can live my life any way I want to," and "If I ruled the world, it would be a better place." Over time, the percentage who scored high had risen substantially.

Mr. Howe and Mr. Strauss had labeled Millennials as "special," which they described as a positive trait, a feeling of self-worth instilled by doting parents. *Generation Me* cast this same feeling in a darker light.

Ms. Twenge even suggested that the rise in volunteering Mr. Howe and Mr. Strauss had described might not indicate an increase in altruism. After all, students knew that doing community service helped them fulfill requirements for the National Honor Society and perhaps get into college. Over time, Ms. Twenge's research created a buzz in higher education, even prompting mention on *Late Night With Conan O'Brien*. Before long, Mr. Howe and Mr. Strauss pounced on her findings, questioning her research and her motivations. In an opinion piece published in *The Christian Science Monitor*, they wrote, "No message ... could be so perverse and contrary to fact as the accusation of selfishness."

Mr. Howe has described Ms. Twenge as having a "Manichaean" view of the world. He has accused her of mistaking self-confidence for narcissism. "You can tell young people that they're not special and see if that works," he says. Colleges and companies alike, he believes, can "leverage" this feeling of specialness among young people and turn it into good things.

Ms. Twenge has stopped short of calling students selfish, but her message has prompted many questions. For one, who is this woman who upset the Millennials' apple cart?

As it turns out, Ms. Twenge is an engaging teacher who draws bell curves on napkins and has no time for nonsense. An associate professor of psychology at San Diego State University, she insists that she likes her students, at least most of them. The ones who ask if they can take final exams early so they can go to Las Vegas, or who grub for grades and demand extra credit? Not so much.

Ms. Twenge's research has given her insights into her personal life. About 10 years ago, she went over the narcissism inventory with a man she was dating. He scored in the 99th percentile, which, she says, confirmed problems in their relationship. After their breakup, she vowed not to end up with the same kind of person. So on her fourth date with another man, she asked him to complete the same questionnaire. He scored low, and they eventually married. She calls the inventory "the boyfriend test" and has given copies to students who want to find out if they're dating a narcissist.

On a Tuesday in August, Ms. Twenge is teaching a course on personality. She arrives a few minutes late because she had to do a radio interview about public perceptions of generations. Today's the last class before the final exam, and students have many questions. One asks if she can get extra points because she listened to Ms. Twenge's interview on the way to class. The answer is no.

While reviewing the semester's lessons, Ms. Twenge walks over to tug on a student's sleeve to demonstrate what a clingy, anxious person might be like in relationship.

Later she introduces some of her research on narcissism. She shows a slide of Whitney Houston from way back and asks if any students remember the singer's 1986 hit "Greatest Love of All." The sight of Ms. Houston's hairdo draws laughter, but Ms. Twenge is serious about one of the song's lyrics—"learning to love yourself is the greatest love of all." In the 1950s, she explains, this very idea would have been beyond weird, but these days, it's normal—and unhealthy. She draws a distinction between self-confidence and narcissism, the latter being associated with a lack of empathy and with aggression after insults.

Ms. Twenge then shows her students a list of statements, such as "Be yourself," "You are special," and "You can be anything you want to be." Then she asks a question: "These phrases are individualistic, but are they good advice?"

"No!" several students say.

"Good," Ms. Twenge replies with a grin. "I've taught you well."

"Are you just being defensively pessimistic?" one student asks.

"Maybe," Ms. Twenge replies.

"Defensive pessimism" is a psychological strategy in which one considers worst-case scenarios and braces for the worst, to avoid disappointment. It's fair description of her, not to mention of her book, says Ms. Twenge, who describes *Generation Me* as a warning about young people, not an indictment of them. "These kids didn't raise themselves," she says. Ms. Twenge tries to practice what she preaches. She does not ask her young daughter, Kate, too many open-ended questions, like "What would you like for dinner?" She does not tell her that she's special, nor does she buy her clothes that say things like "Little Princess."

Ms. Twenge does, however, take her along on speaking trips. This year she has given about 15 presentations, for which she charges between $1,000 and $5,000. Recently she has spoken at PepsiCo, McGraw-Hill, and the Florida Association of Blood Banks, where she encouraged attendees to appeal to young peoples' sense that they can make a personal difference by donating their blood—"Make it about them." During her presentations, she asks her audience to sing along to a song that's become popular in preschools. It's a song she dislikes. Sung to the tune of "Frère Jacques," it goes, "I am special, I am special, look at me, look at me. ..."

Teenagers who grow up with this chorus in their heads have a venue for self-absorption that their parents never imagined. It's called the Internet. Ms. Twenge argues that Facebook and other social media have fed a bonfire of vanity among young people. On the other side of the country, a scholar named Mark Bauerlein has reached a similar conclusion.

Mr. Bauerlein, an English professor at Emory University, in Atlanta, is the author of *The Dumbest Generation: How the Digital Age Stupefies Young Americans and Jeopardizes Our Future*. The sub-subtitle turns an old generational rallying cry on its head: "Don't trust anyone under 30."

Mr. Bauerlein (who writes for *The Chronicle Review*'s Brainstorm blog) concerns himself with only one generational trait, what he calls the "intellectual condition." Today's students, though blessed with limitless high-tech wonders, have squandered these tools, using computers mostly for their amusement—chatting, networking, and posting online updates about themselves, Mr. Bauerlein argues. Teenagers, he writes, "are drowning in their own ignorance and aliteracy." To tout the technological skills of today's students, he continues, "feeds the generational consciousness that keeps kids from growing up."

Mr. Bauerlein, 50, directed the survey reported in "Reading at Risk: A Survey of Literary Reading in America," published by the National Endowment for the Arts in 2004. It found a sharp decline in reading among all age groups between 1982 and 2002, and the largest drop was among people between 18 and 24. In *The Dumbest Generation*, he cited numerous other studies that affirmed that today's students were reading less and absorbing fewer facts than their predecessors had. His own experiences in the class-room also informed his conclusions. He describes most of his students as highly professional; he encounters fewer and fewer who seem interested in culture, in wrestling with ideas. "Many of them have a mercenary attitude about the university, and they regard humanities as an interruption," he says. In this, he foresees cultural doom.

Not long ago, Mr. Bauerlein faced off against Mr. Howe in Washington during a debate sponsored by the American Enterprise Institute. He thinks Mr. Howe has many good insights, but he sees limits to them. "There's an investment in being enthusiastic—maybe too strong an investment in that," Mr. Bauerlein says.

Like Ms. Twenge, Mr. Bauerlein describes his book as a labor of love, not scorn. "It's a provocation with a generous aim," he says. "In the raising and rearing of young people, a critical voice is essential. They have to hear someone knock them down, and if they fight back, that's good. It's part of the health of a culture from generation to generation." Several technophiles in academe have cast Mr. Bauerlein as a Luddite who clings to a single (and dated) definition of literacy. He invites them to his classes. "They've never sat across from a freshman who comes in and says, 'I don't want to read any novel.' It's a lot easier to be sanguine about students if you've never encountered that."

The professor acknowledges that the book's title is incendiary. As his agent assured him, bold proclamations help get authors on the radar, though his conclusions are more nuanced than the cover might suggest. Still, when he told his wife that he planned to dedicate the book to her, she said no thanks. She knew that a book that called roughly 100 million people dumb would make him a public enemy. Sure enough, since the book came out last year, Mr. Bauerlein has received scores of angry e-mail messages, many of them from teenagers. Recently, a 13-year-old wrote that he was "great, big hypocrite." Another began: "Dear sir, you are an ass."

A curious thing has happened, though. Mr. Bauerlein, who says that he has responded to each message he has received, has become engaged in several positive, continuing dialogues with some of the parents and students who wrote to him. It's a testament to the possibilities of the very technology he has questioned. As the Millennial decade rolled on, Mr. Bauerlein and other professors encountered waves of teenagers who had grown up using search engines and instant messaging, and they wondered how those experiences might affect the way students learned. Many students were indeed behaving more like fussy consumers. It was not clear how far their demands would go for personalization, satisfaction, and instant gratification. This uncertainty led to a larger question about supposed generational traits. Were educators to see them as something to indulge—or to cure?

Many instructors who weighed this question with regard to technology have tried to meet students where they are, by incorporating Facebook, Twitter, and all kinds of multimedia platforms into their teaching. Siva Vaidhyanathan has no problem with such innovation per se, but he questions the notion that regardless of what they are teaching, instructors must do all they can to please Millennials by embracing technological portals like some kind of magical device. "There's this expectation that your No. 1 job is to pander to this exotic alien consumer," says Mr. Vaidhyanathan, an associate professor of media studies at the University of Virginia. "At that point, you cease being a teacher and you are simply selling yourself to an audience that might not be interested in buying."

Mr. Vaidhyanathan has read *Millennials Rising*. He says Mr. Howe and Mr. Strauss might as well have written a book on how to reach out to Geminis. "If you work in higher education, the first thing you should do is throw out all their books," says Mr. Vaidhyanathan. "Generational thinking is just a benign form of bigotry, in which you flatten out diversity. This is debilitating to the job of trying to work with young people."

Over the last decade, commentators have tended to slap the Millennial label on white, affluent teenagers who accomplish great things as they grow up in the suburbs, who confront anxiety when applying to super-selective colleges, and who multitask with ease as their helicopter parents hover reassuringly above them. The label tends not to appear in renderings of teenagers who happen to

CRITICAL PERSPECTIVES ON MILLENNIALS

be minorities, or poor, or who have never won a spelling bee. Nor does the term often refer to students from big cities and small towns that are nothing like Fairfax County, Va. Or who lack technological know-how. Or who struggle to complete high school. Or who never even consider college. Or who commit crimes. Or who suffer from too little parental support. Or who drop out of college. Aren't they Millennials, too?

Many pieces of the Millennial puzzle are missing, says Fred A. Bonner II. He's one of several researchers who have examined the experiences of nonwhite students in hopes of broadening the understanding of the generation.

Mr. Bonner, an associate professor in the department of educational administration and human resources at Texas A&M University, has described how the prevailing generational descriptions focus narrowly on the experiences of majority populations. He believes the Howe/Strauss model is useful, but limited. "Many other kinds of students have not come from backgrounds where they felt safe, sheltered, and secure, or from schools that recognized their gifts and talents," says Mr. Bonner, who is 40.

During class discussions, he has listened to black and Hispanic students describe how some or all of the so-called seven core traits did not apply to them. They often say the "special" trait, in particular, is unrecognizable. "It's not that many diverse parents don't want to treat their kids as special," he says, "but they often don't have the social and cultural capital, the time and resources, to do that."

Mr. Bonner is a co-editor of a forthcoming book, tentatively titled *Diverse Millennials in College*, which Stylus Publishing plans to publish in 2010. In recent years, Mr. Bonner has also done some generational consulting of his own. So far that work has been limited to speaking engagements at two- and four-year colleges. Generally his audiences understand that the experiences of a black Millennial from, say, Houston may differ greatly from the experiences of a white student from the Houston suburbs. After all, people who work in higher education see plenty of reminders that the *when* of a student's birth is but one factor in that student's development. Where a student is born, who a student's parents are, and how much money they have—all these things influence that student's educational opportunities, scores on standardized tests, and expectations of college.

"Some folks are using this as a template and a cookbook," Mr. Bonner says of Millennials descriptions. "It makes it very difficult to see and understand variations because people who don't fit the recipe may be viewed as outliers. That anesthetizes nuances."

At the same time, generalizations are often as necessary as lifeboats; they allow people to navigate a sea of complexity. This is the very reason that many people in higher education have found Mr. Howe so useful.

The list of those who swear by his work is long. One is Lisa A. Rossbacher, president of Southern Polytechnic State University, in Georgia. After hearing Mr. Howe at a conference a year ago, she invited him to come talk to faculty and staff members on her campus recently. The university has made many changes that incorporate his insights into Millennials. To acknowledge their comfort with technology, it offers more hybrid courses that combine classroom and online learning. To satisfy their wish for more feedback, it encourages instructors to assign more group work and more short, graded assignments. To involve their parents, it provides them with cellphone numbers for the vice presidents for students affairs and for enrollment.

Those are all changes that the university probably would have made anyway, Ms. Rossbacher suspects, only without knowing exactly why. "We can see the trends, but Neil gives us the context to help us understand why we're seeing the things we are seeing," she says. "He speaks as an outside authority, as a prophet not in his own land."

Among other things, Mr. Howe is a gifted storyteller. He describes generational membership as an underappreciated part of people's stories, but concedes that it's just one part. So perhaps his conclusions about the generations are best thought of as medieval maps, with their rough approximations of a land's boundaries and rivers. They suggest a general features, though they do not give you all the specifics you would need to get somewhere. Like inside a particular student's head.

These days Mr. Howe's talking about the next birth cohort, born 2005-25, which he calls the "Homeland Generation." According to his framework, those Americans will fit an "artist" archetype. "Such generations tend to be remembered for their quiet years of rising adulthood," he has written, "and their midlife years of flexible, consensus-building leadership." One day Mr. Howe hopes to start a nonprofit group devoted to the study of generational differences. After all, historians may never fully embrace it.

"Academia gives this no home despite the fact that managers of for-profits and nonprofits find it so valuable," Mr. Howe says. "Why is it that I constantly get calls? This is a demand-driven business."

It's a business that begets business. In the Millennials industry, plenty of people owe their success—not to mention their talking points—to Mr. Howe. If you're a career counselor on a college campus, odds are good that many of your students go on to work for companies that have paid experts to come and explain how to make young workers happy and retain them. Perhaps the expert was Mary Crane, who was once a lobbyist, then an assistant chef at the White House, before becoming a full-time generational consultant for Fortune 500 companies and law firms. Recently she was featured on a *60 Minutes* segment about Millennials. Or perhaps it was Eric Greenberg, a philanthropist who found the time to write a book called *Generation We: How Millennial Youth Are Taking Over America and Changing Our World Forever* in between running Beautifull Inc., a health-food company, and endowing genetics laboratories.

Lynne Lancaster, a management consultant and "cultural translator," is a co-founder and partner of BridgeWorks LLC, which offers companies advice on bridging generational divides among employees. So does Kanna Hudson, 26, a former academic counselor who works for a consulting company called Futurist. com. Another consultant, Scott Degraffenreid, a former forensic accountant, wrote *Understanding the Millennial Mind: A Menace or Amazing?* and patented the term "crash-test geniuses" to refer to young people's willingness to "reboot" and learn from failures, even if it means walking away from their jobs. Eric Chester, a former teacher, runs a consulting business called Generation Why; his Web site describes young people as "weird-looking and impossible to understand."

Such descriptions are reminders that most renderings of Millennials are done by older people, looking through the windows of their own experiences. So in any discussion of generations, it's only fair to give a Millennial the last word. This is tricky exercise, however. After all, it's easy to find one who agrees—or disagrees—with the idea that students are team-oriented, or narcissistic, or anything. And many have given generational labels no more consideration than the ingredients of their breakfast cereal.

Susanna Wolff, however, has thought a lot about the differences between younger and older people, at least in terms of their mastery of technology, a theme she mines for laughs. Ms. Wolff, a senior at Columbia University, compiles a weekly feature called "Parents Just Don't Understand," for collegehumor.com, a popular Web site. Submissions come from all over the country, about mothers who don't understand how e-mail works and fathers who ask about joining "MyFace."

Besides technology, however, Ms. Wolff believes that people her age have few common experiences to bind them together the way Millennial theories describe. When she hears the term "Millennial," she thinks of marketing executives huddled around tables, looking at pie charts and figuring out how to sell stuff. "When every commercial is marketed to you," she says, "it feeds the idea that everything revolves around you."

Ms. Wolff sees many things that complicate generational generalizations. Take her own family. Although she's close to her parents, they call her more than she calls them. In fact, she talks most often to her grandmother—who recently sought her advice on starting a blog.

Although she is wary of the many predictions about her generation, Ms. Wolff, 21, offers a guess about what people her age will be like in, say, 20 years. "We'll be really good at the technology we're familiar with and really bad about learning anything new," she says. "And we'll complain about the young people."

1. What challenges have millennials posed to higher education? How have universities responded to these challenges?

2. Howe and Strauss said that millennials would rebel by changing the world. What evidence can you find that this is true? What evidence can you find that this is false?

"MILLENNIALS V BABY BOOMERS: A BATTLE WE COULD HAVE DONE WITHOUT," BY STEVEN ROBERTS AND KIM ALLEN, FROM *THE CONVERSATION*, APRIL 6, 2016

The generation of young people who came of age during the new millennium – "millennials", as they're commonly known – has divided opinion like no other. Some have deemed them a self-pitying and entitled bunch; lazy, deluded and narcissistic. Others take a more sympathetic view, raising concerns that millennials are at risk of becoming a "lost generation". After all, they are making the transition into adulthood under much more precarious circumstances than their parents experienced as part of the "baby boomers" generation.

The challenges millennials face include the rising costs of education; an increased likelihood of unemployment and underemployment – even for a growing number of graduates – and falling incomes even when they are employed. For millennials, home ownership is an increasingly distant prospect, and private rents are soaring. To top it all off, young people have been hit particularly hard by benefit sanctions and cuts to public sector funding.

Since the global financial crisis, the supposed plight of the millennials has given rise to the argument that inequality is an age-related issue: young people are disadvantaged, while baby boomers collectively prosper at their expense. This idea is exemplified by the Guardian's recent series on millennials, and perpetuated by other outlets. With austerity and weak economic growth ensuring that the opportunities for younger people are comparatively diminished, even academics are raising "the issue of youth-as-class".

FACING THE CHANGES

We don't deny that the experience of being young has changed significantly. But this notion of a single millennial experience deserves some serious questioning. While young people are encountering changes – and often challenges – in terms of employment, education and housing, they do not all experience this hostile landscape in the same way.

By talking about "the millennials" as a disadvantaged group, we're in danger of obscuring other, more fundamental differences between young people. For example, class background is still a particularly important determinant of a young person's life chances. Our own research – as well as the work of many others – demonstrates the importance of parental support for young people transitioning into adulthood.

Having a room in the family home or access to other family finances is key to undertaking unpaid internships or volunteer work. A monthly allowance from your folks while at university facilitates access to important CV building activities, which top graduate employers seek from applicants. It ensures that during your exams you don't have to carry on looking for a job, and it helps you to avoid the choice between eating or heating.

Gifting or loaning deposits for a rented or purchased home is still a middle-class practice. There are many other ways that parents can, and do, use their resources to help their children onto the property ladder.

CLASS STRUGGLE

So, while middle-class young people are clearly facing difficulties during their transition to independence, they are also more likely to have access to resources that are unavailable to their less-advantaged peers, which help to reduce risks and protect them from uncertainties. These resources help young people to "weather the storm" and influence who survives and prospers in the current conditions.

Let us recall some other significant class-based advantages: higher education remains very stratified, and those attending elite research-intensive institutions are disproportionately middle class. Children of middle-class parents earn more than peers of working class origins, even when they obtain employment in top jobs. And while baby-boomers may be holding onto the housing stock for now, the children of the property-owning middle classes will one day inherit it.

As well as class, research has long shown how gender, race, disability and a host of other factors work to shape a person's future. More recent evidence suggests that the financial crisis and subsequent austerity have had a particularly disproportionate effect on women, certain black and minority ethnic groups and the disabled.

What's more, proclaiming an inter-generational war unhelpfully clouds the fact that the prospects for certain groups of older people are just as bad – if not worse – than for many young people. Despite the dominant media image of the resource-rich retiree, many older people do not have comfortable pensions, homes or savings to fall back on. And as the state withdraws funding for public services such as social care, older women have been forced to step in and undertake unpaid labour by caring for elderly family members.

Declarations of inter-generational conflict between baby boomers and millennials might grab headlines. But the real story is the same as it ever was; that our society is plagued by long-standing, ongoing inequalities relating to class, race and gender. The portrayal of millennials as victims has allowed the experience of the squeezed middle class to take centre stage. Now, it's up to us to question who's really at a disadvantage in our society – and how we can make life fairer for all.

1. Do you believe that younger generations can largely be grouped against older generations by their socio-economic status? Why or why not?

2. How would you answer this question at the end of the article: "Who's really at a disadvantage in our society—and how can we make life fairer for all?"

CHAPTER 2

MILLENNIALS AND POLITICS

Many millennials came of age at a time of turmoil, with the United States fighting wars in the Middle East, a global recession that impacted their ability to get jobs, and student debt that made upward mobility a challenge. This shaped millennials' views on politics, making some disillusioned with the political system. But they have also proven themselves a force to be reckoned with; young voters were among the key supporters that brought President Barack Obama into office and helped shape the way politicians use social media. In this chapter, we'll hear from politicians on both sides of the aisle on how they view millennials, as well as look at research on how millennials engage with the political system and how they can shape the politics of the future.

"WHY I'M BETTING ON YOU TO HELP SHAPE THE NEW AMERICAN ECONOMY," BY BARACK OBAMA, FROM THE WHITE HOUSE VIA MEDIUM, OCTOBER 9, 2014

You're part of the first generation to grow up in the digital age. Some of you grew up with cell phones tucked into your book bags, while others can remember the early days of landline, dial-up internet. You've gone from renting movies on VHS tapes to purchasing and downloading them in a matter of minutes.

Today, more of you are earning college degrees than ever before—and more young people from low-income families are getting a shot at higher education than previous generations. Along with having higher education levels, you've got a lower gender pay gap than other generations—and we're working to close it even further. Take all those things together, and it's no surprise that entrepreneurship is in your DNA. One survey found that more than half of Millennials expressed interest in starting (or have already started) their own business.

And we know that when we invest in your potential, rather than stack the deck in favor of the folks who are already at the top, our entire economy does better. It's the reason we've expanded grants, tax credits, and loans to help more families afford college. It's why we're giving nearly 5 million Americans the chance to cap student loan payments at 10 percent of their income. And thanks to the Affordable Care Act, the number of uninsured young adults has fallen by nearly 40 percent over the past four years.

You may have graduated into the worst recession since the Great Depression, but today—for all the challenges you've already faced, and after all the grueling work it's taken to bounce back—you're in the best position to break into the newest sectors of the new American economy.

Your generation is going to continue to shape that economy for decades to come—and that's exactly why we know we have more work to do to address the challenges you still face. That means making student loan payments even more affordable. It means investing in the kind of basic research that led to the internet and GPS technology to help our next generation of American companies succeed. And at a time when increased investments in education have meant that young women are making the strongest start in the workforce of any generation before them, it means fighting to make sure they get the equal pay for equal work they deserve.

Let's talk for a second about this new American economy—one marked by new industry and commerce, humming with new energy and new technology, and being driven forward by highly skilled, higher-wage workers. Our medical professionals are part of a workforce that also includes folks who are developing cutting-edge software to help us diagnose diseases. We're not just punching in and pounding rivets—we're coding computers and guiding robots. In this new economy, an entrepreneur can start a new business and succeed, an older worker who sees opportunity in a new field has resources available to retool for that new job, and a student can graduate from college with the chance to advance through a vibrant job market.

Today, I'm heading to a place that's helping to shape that economy. It's called Cross Campus—a collaborative space in Los Angeles that brings together folks at the cutting edge of a technology revolution, from investors and entrepreneurs to designers and engineers. Because their drive and talent don't just boost their businesses, they boost our entire economy—and the innovative ideas that they're coming up with are helping to power our recovery.

Think about this: Last month, our businesses created 236,000 new jobs. Over the past 55 months, they've created 10.3 million new jobs—the longest uninterrupted stretch of private-sector job creation in our history. That's why, for the first time in more than six years, the unemployment rate is below 6 percent. We're on pace for the strongest year of job growth since the 1990s. Since we emerged from the crisis, America has put more people back to work than Europe, Japan, and every other advanced economy combined.

So for all the challenges in the world, there are some really good things going on here at home. And the reason I'm heading to Cross Campus today is because innovation is one of them. Technologies that didn't exist 20 years ago, from mobile apps to streaming video to social networks, support millions of American jobs today. Today, our tech sector is the envy of the world.

I saw this new economy at Pittsburgh's TechShop, one in a chain of community centers where members get access to professional tools, equipment, and software, as well as the space they need to make or design or proto-type almost anything—for the same price you'd pay for a gym membership.

I saw this new economy at a factory in Austin, where workers are building the equipment that makes cutting-edge microchips. It was just a few years ago that the very first iPhone was introduced, and we were all marveling over touch screens. Now, even our coffee shops have touch-screen ordering systems, and there are American workers punching in every day to manufacture the hardware for our smartphones and tablets.

And I saw this new economy only a few miles from that factory, at Manor New Tech High School. Students there focus on STEM subjects, and I got to see some of their work up close—from using mathematical equations to build musical instruments, to running bungee-jumping tests using rubber bands and weights, to building robots. At Manor New Tech, nearly all of the students graduate, and along with their diploma, they've earned real-world skills they need to fill the jobs we know are available right now.

Throughout my time in office, my Administration has bet on American innovation. We've bet on America's young people. And today, I'm betting that you'll continue unleashing new ideas and new enterprises for decades to come.

1. What might millennials offer the economy that past generations have not?

2. What did the Obama administration do to help millennials make their mark on the economy?

"FULL REMARKS: SPEAKER RYAN HOLDS MILLENNIAL TOWN HALL AT GEORGETOWN," BY SPEAKER PAUL RYAN, FROM *PAUL RYAN: SPEAKER OF THE HOUSE*, APRIL 27, 2016

WASHINGTON — Today, House Speaker Paul Ryan (R-WI) held a town hall with millennials at the Georgetown Institute of Politics and Public Service, where he made the case for why young people should believe in conservatism. Speaker Ryan began the town hall by delivering remarks, followed by Q&A with students in the audience and participating online. Below are Speaker Ryan's full opening remarks as prepared for delivery:

John, Kayla—thank you for the introduction. A special thanks to S. E. Cupp for inviting me—and to all of you here for indulging me. I look forward to answering your questions. But first, I want to make my case: why support Republicans. I'm going to go out on a limb and assume the thought had not occurred to most of you. So here's how I'd sum it up. The America that you want is the America that we want: open, diverse, dynamic. It is what I call a confident America, where the condition of your birth does not determine the outcome of your life—where we tackle our problems together so that all of us can thrive.

How do we get there? How do we do that? That is why I am here today.

Building that America is the reason that I got into politics, though I never thought I'd run for office when I was your age. Back then, I wanted to be an economist, which goes to show just how much fun I was in those days. But my last year in college, I got offered a job on Capitol Hill, where I had interned the summer before. And, seniors, you're learning this just now: The first time anybody offers to hire you for anything, it is a huge relief—and somewhat of a shock.

But I almost didn't take it. What I really wanted to do was to go to Colorado and spend a few years enjoying the outdoors. I thought I'd climb mountains and wait tables in the summer—and in the winter I'd join the ski patrol. Well, when I mentioned this idea to my mom, she wasn't exactly enthusiastic. She said to me, 'If you do that, you'll just become a ski bum. One year will turn into three, three into six, and before you know it, you'll be 30 years old'— which, to 22-year-old me, sounded ancient.

So I took the job. And I quickly realized that public service was where I could have the biggest impact. You could make a real difference in people's lives—and at a young age. So when the congressman who represented my district decided to leave the House, I ran for his seat. I was just 28 years old. And to everybody's surprise— myself included—I won.

I went into politics because I wanted to solve problems. I entered Congress in 1999. I don't even want to know how old all of you were back then. But it was a different time. Cell phones were a lot bigger—and so was my hair. And the hot-button issue was Social Security. I got involved because I wanted to save it. For me, it was personal.

My dad died when I was 16, so my family relied on his Social Security survivor benefits. I used them to help pay for college. My mom used them to help her start a new career. She had just turned 50, and now she had to start over. So every weekday, she'd get on a bus and ride 40 miles to Madison to go to school. She was able to learn new skills and start a small business. So I knew what Social Security had done for my family. And I wanted all Americans—of all generations—to have that same level of security.

But this speaks to a larger point. When I was growing up, I lived in a country where if you got up every day and gave it your all, it would pay off. You could find a rewarding job. You could start your own business. You could buy a home and raise a family in a nice neighborhood. And no matter where you came from, no office or distinction was too high for your reach. Anything was possible, if you were willing to make the effort. And if life threw you a curve ball, you would get the support you needed.

That, I think, is the kind of country we all want to live in. And you know better than most that it doesn't just happen automatically. You grew up during the Great Recession. You saw for yourselves how opportunity can disappear in a moment. When I talk to college graduates these days, it's clear they're still living with the consequences of the crash. They studied hard, but they can't find a job that matches their skills. They're working hard, but they're not getting that promotion they hoped for. They want to buy a house, but they can't afford it. They want to save for retirement, but they can't sacrifice the money.

So the question is, how do we open up opportunity for everyone in this country? And what, specifically, is the government's role here? As you might have heard, this is a matter of dispute. And it has been for some time.

I just want to say my Democratic friends are good people who love their country. I work with them every day to find common ground and make progress where we can. But there are real disagreements between us. And *we should be clear about them—because then, when the time comes, the people can decide which way they want to go. And I believe many of our current policies are shutting young people out of our economy by taking decisions away from people—from the individual.*

This is the difference: We do not believe we should be governed by our betters—that elites in Washington should make all the big decisions—that they should pick winners and losers—that's a recipe for a closed economy—for cronyism. We want an open economy where there's equal opportunity for all ... where more people can participate and rise by their talents ... where the individual can put their ideas and their aspirations to the test.

This contrast can be hard to visualize, so here's an example.

Say you have an idea for a new business, and you want to create a startup. Well, you need to raise money. And if you want to raise money on the Internet—as many people do—you typically have two options: Ask for donations or loans. But there's also a third option: Offer stock. Sounds intimidating, but it's not really. It's basically just crowdsourcing for investors. And it works for a lot of people because when you're not making money, you don't owe your investors anything—unlike debt. But a few years ago, the Securities and Exchange Commission got involved. It thought this kind of crowdfunding was too risky for small-dollar investors—that is, people like you—and said they couldn't do it. Instead of laying down rules to make it safe—so people like you could participate—the SEC ruled it out of bounds. That's the difference between giving information to people and making decisions for them.

That's why we passed a law to make the SEC change course. We said, 'Write rules so more people can participate. Don't outlaw it.' And what happened? More people got to invest, and more start-ups got to expand. Now, we're still working out the kinks in the law. We're actually considering a bill this week. But I would argue that this shows the kind of mindset we need in government. The point of having rules is to open up opportunity, not to shut it off. It is to give people the information they need so they can take action. It is that information that turns you into an investor or an inventor or an entrepreneur. And that's how we solve problems in this country—from the bottom up, not the top down. Now we need to take this mindset and apply it to the challenges of the day. Here are just a few more examples …

I'm all for helping people pay for health insurance. But the health care law literally outlawed millions of plans that were working. And now millions are struggling to pay their premiums. If you're young and healthy, you don't need a plan with all the bells and whistles. You just need basic coverage. So why not open up our health care system so people can pick a plan that works for them?

Student debt is now bigger than credit card debt. And so many of my friends on the other side say we should make community college free. But what if you don't want to go to community college? Why don't we break up the college cartel and let students try different options? Why don't we give our students a choice?

We've been fighting the War on Poverty for over 50 years now. We spend billions of dollars each year on 92 different programs. And yet poverty is not all that much lower than when we started. But if you look in our local communities, there are actually thousands of people fighting poverty on the front lines every day—and winning. Instead of trying to replace them, why doesn't government support them?

There are over 2 million people in our prisons. Many of them are not hardened criminals. They're not violent. A lot of them are just people who made a mistake. I think we need to let more people earn a second chance at life. Instead of locking people up, why don't we unlock their potential?

The good news is, we don't just have to ask these questions. We can do these things. That is why, right now, Republicans are working on a policy agenda to address some of the challenges I have discussed here today. If we do not like the direction our country is going—and we do not— then we owe the country an alternative. We owe it to you.

I know you have heard people like me say that yours may be the first generation to be left worse off than the one before it. That does not have to happen, and it will not have to happen if we seize this moment.

Maybe this will help sum up things up. At the Democrats' national convention in 2012, they showed a video that said, 'Government's the only thing that we all belong to.' I think they had it exactly backward. Government is the only thing that belongs to all of us. It is not supposed to manage the people, but to serve them. And I think this mindset is totally in sync with the way you live your lives. It's almost a cliché to say your generation is the most technologically savvy we've ever seen. If I can log in to Netflix—that's a win for me. And you know better than anyone that technology is not a toy or distraction. It is what allows you to focus on the essentials: faith, family, work. I would argue government is supposed to do the same thing.

These days, with technology, you are used to customizing your everyday life. So why on earth would you want to support a governing philosophy that seeks to take away your right and ability to customize, individualize, or decide critical aspects of your life, like your health care or your education? You can't say government is of the people when it is imposing its decisions on the people.

Government does not impose community. The people create it—and government's role is to protect it. Only we the people can build a confident America. So today I am asking for your help. We need your ideas. We need you to create the next Uber or Lyft or Twitter or Snapchat … or to raise the next generation … or to run for office … or to get involved in our community … or do all of these things.

Because that's who we are—a country that sees the potential in every human being and does everything we can to bring that potential to life. Thank you.

1. What are some of the most important issues Speaker Ryan feels millennials face today? How do these issues impact the country as a whole?

2. The article notes that some reproductive rights activists prefer to reframe "choice" as "justice." What do you think of this shift?

"MILLENNIALS' NON-VOTING HABITS, EXPLAINED," BY KATE ARONOFF, FROM *COMMON DREAMS*, MAY 08, 2016

What's the matter with millennials? The latest person to ask and answer this question is Vox's David Roberts. Listing out a series of polls explaining how supportive 18-29-year-olds are of climate action and clean energy, Roberts reaches a crossroads: If millennials care so much about global warming, then why aren't they doing anything about it?

"The problem is, too few of them vote," he says, pointing to low voter turn-outs in the last few elections.

The article itself is filled with cheeky stock photos of millennials taking selfies and walking around college campus sporting vests and fedoras. Look at all the stylish fun they're having while not voting! Millennials, for Roberts, are a perplexing but — ultimately — useful herd of sheep in need of a good shepherd.

The man for the job, says Roberts, is Very Serious Man Tom Steyer, a hedge fund billionaire and top donor to liberal candidates and causes. He founded NextGen Climate and its associated PAC to bring millennials out to the polls, tapping into their widespread support for stopping climate catastrophe. NextGen was founded in 2013 and is now launching a $25 million campaign to "register and mobilize young voters in seven key battleground states to help elect climate champions to the White House and the Senate this fall."

While going into detail on NextGen's plans for the coming months, Roberts somehow gets through a (not-short) piece on millennials, voting and the 2016 election without once mentioning Bernie Sanders, the candidate who has captured double-digit leads among that demographic — even in states that he's lost. Millennials would even choose a dinner with Sanders over one with Beyonce or Justin Bieber.

Perhaps more surprisingly, Roberts doesn't bring up the millennials who've already pushed the climate conversation this election into the mainstream, cornering Clinton into a firm rejection of the Keystone XL pipeline and prompting a national conversation about the role of fossil fuel money — including hers — in politics. Also absent are the now hundreds of students who've been arrested to stop the Keystone XL pipeline, and the over 60 of them jailed this spring for fossil fuel divestment.

These are serious gaps, but relatively standard from the pundits who've built a cottage industry on making bad predictions about this election — largely by under-estimating the importance of political outsiders. But if Bernie Sanders and Donald Trump's surprising success has shown anything, it's that political elites are more subject than ever to outside forces, and movements. Roberts isn't alone in leaving the grassroots out of the picture of this election. Winning on climate, though — at the scale science demands — requires a more holistic understanding of the political arena than simply voting and non-voting. Why, beyond the Sanders campaign, haven't millennials been engaged en mass in elections in traditional ways? What are they doing instead?

As a younger millennial, here are a few #MillennialFacts — in Roberts's words — to help explain what's happening in 2016, and why my generation has such a complicated relationship to the ballot box.

I was born in 1992, meaning my first real memories of the Oval Office are of Bill Clinton. Not of NATO bombings or crime bills, but of Monica Lewinsky and the Starr Report. I was too young to understand the controversy that marked the 2000 election, but old enough to know I shouldn't like the guy who came out on top or the process that put him there.

Before reaching double digits, two planes had hit the Twin Towers and the Bush administration had launched us into a war that's followed me into adulthood, the reasoning for which I don't understand any better now than when I was learning algebra. Two years later we entered another war I understood even less — that one sending my brother on a brief and thankfully uneventful tour in Iraq. No Child Left Behind gifted my mother with the task of preparing her special education students for tests she and the school both know they couldn't pass. The 2004 election inexplicably brought on four more years of Bush. So, by the time there was a chance to elect someone I was actually excited about, I knocked on doors in the hopes of something different, even if I couldn't yet vote myself. The millennials who could vote came out in record numbers for Obama in 2008, and thousands organized for the campaign. Maybe — just maybe — he could dig us out of a nasty recession and perpetual, bloody conflict in the Middle East.

By the time I was old enough to actually vote for Obama, though, the hope and change that colored his election had faded. Rather than sweeping progressive reform, we got a more tech savvy version of the same wars, and an economic recovery that brought my generation's economic prospects to a deflated and precarious new normal; five-figure student debt was ready to greet me at graduation.

It should be said, too, that I was lucky. My family's assets remained largely intact after the crash. Black households, by comparison, saw their wealth decline by a full 31 percent between 2007 and 2010. I also wasn't subject to the round-the-clock surveillance that's stalked Muslim communities since the advent of the Patriot Act. Nor do I have loved ones incarcerated by the War on Drugs or deported by draconian immigration policies.

In the midst of all this disappointment, it wasn't a call for four more years of the same that inspired me. It was the scrappy, stubborn millennials who decided to camp out in public parks around the country. Fraught as Occupy was — and it was plenty fraught — it stood for something electoral politics never had: a better future, and the radical demand for a world without want or rule by the 1 percent. I was too young and too suburban to be a part of the anti-war movement, so Occupy first showed me what it could look like for people, not politicians, to shape a national conversation. It even managed to turn Mitt Romney's background in private equity from a selling point to a liability, painting him as the candidate of, by and for the elite. The years since 2011 and 2012 have seen an uptick in similarly transformative movements, most recently in the movement for black lives.

For good reason, then, millennials have placed more faith in protests than in politicians. But Roberts's data isn't wrong: Millennials don't vote at the levels we should, even as we rally behind Sanders's Occupy-inspired campaign. Next-Gen's work on this front is important; getting more millennials out to the polls is vital. And though Steyer has a penchant for taking chummy pictures with Koch brothers and dissing activists, he's funding a project that needs to exist.

At the same time, however, it's also no magic bullet for cracking the seemingly impenetrable nut of millennial civic engagement — let alone to getting the kind of comprehensive climate policy and energy system overhaul that Roberts outlines so skillfully in his other writing. In its mildest form, adequate climate action means a dramatic reimagining of America's economic and political system, both in terms of the story we tell about them and the people in charge. (That might be one reason why some 43 percent of millennials favor socialism and 51 percent reject the capitalism that's wrecked our paychecks, planet and political system.)

To beat a familiar drum, social movements and upheavals are the driving force behind transformative political shifts and realignments. Climate will be no different. Where NextGen can ensure that millennials show up to vote, movements determine who and what goes on the ballot. The political weather that movements help create determines everything from the kinds of candidates running to the policies they're feasibly able to push. Of course, it's a street that runs both ways: Just as Occupy laid the groundwork for Bernie Sanders's candidacy in 2008's wake, the Tea Party — in its years of dedicated grassroots organizing — has paved the way for Trump. It wasn't FDR, after all, who created the foundation for a bolstered welfare state after the Great Depression. It was the armies of the unemployed, who marched tens-of-thousands strong on Washington and congressional districts around the country.

Knowing all this, millennial movements have developed an increasingly nuanced understanding of the interplay between protests and politics. Their leaders, emboldened — but not limited by — the Sanders campaign, are exploring the prospects of independent political power. Us millennials want a new kind of politics to vote for, and are already building it — not because we feel entitled to it, but because it's our collective best shot at a livable future.

1. According to the author, what are some of the issues millennials care the most about? What issues not mentioned here do you think are important to millennials?

2. How would you describe the millennial view of politics, and how does this impact their opinions on voting?

"WHAT YOU NEED TO KNOW ABOUT MILLENNIALS AND POLITICS," BY ELIZABETH CAMPBELL, NATALIE GRIFFIN, AND AMBER REECE, FROM *NEWS 21*, AUGUST 24, 2016

PHOENIX — Millennials get a bad rap when it comes to voting. They're labeled narcissistic, self-absorbed and apathetic. (Just look at their nicknames: the selfie generation, generation me, the unemployables.)

And they're the least likely generation to turn up at the polls this November.

However, many young Americans do care about politics. They may just show it differently than their more-traditional parents.

As of April, the U.S. Census Bureau estimated there were about 69.2 million millennials, roughly defined as Americans age 18 to 35, in the U.S. electorate, according to a Pew Research Center study. This group makes up about a third of the voting-age population, matching the baby boomers.

And that means they have the potential to strongly influence upcoming elections. But will they? Here's what you need to know about millennials and voting.

THEY DIFFER FROM PREVIOUS GENERATIONS, BOTH SOCIALLY AND POLITICALLY

Millennials are more diverse than any generation before them. According to 2014 census data, 44 percent of them identify as nonwhite.

Elli Denison, director of research for the Center for Generational Kinetics, a Texas-based consulting firm that specializes in generational research, said millennials have grown up with diversity and celebrate it.

"They really value that," Denison said. "They look at a group of people and think 'Oh, dear, we all look the same.'" And that troubles them.

Mike Hais, co-author of the book "Millennial Majority: How a New Coalition is Remaking American Politics," agreed. He said this diversity has led to the generation being more accepting, which affects their political views.

"They tend to be the most socially tolerant generation in America," Hais said. "Immigration, gay rights and the like, for all these reasons, their attitudes tend to be progressive and tolerant. They really are, in that sense, a very distinctive generation."

Those distinctions doesn't always correlate along party lines, either. According to a 2016 Gallup poll, 44 percent of millennials identify as independents, while 28 percent identify as Democrats and 19 percent Republicans.

Hais also called the millennials "the most female-driven generation in American history" thanks to high enrollment numbers for women in college. In 2015, about 11.5 million women were expected to attend colleges and universities, compared with 8.7 million men, according to the National Center for Educational Statistics.

Joan Kuhl, founder of the site WhyMillennials-Matter.com, said the millennial generation is "the most educated generation yet."

But the increases in educational attainment comes at a price. This generation has high levels of college debt, another factor in the millennial puzzle, Kuhl said. It's also a reason, she said, this generation gets saddled with the "entitled" label.

"'Entitled' is misunderstanding the debt piece," Kuhl said. "They say, 'I want financial security. I want steady increases in pay because I want to get my feet on the ground, not because I want to spend it on silly things.'

"The people who are most offended by millennials acting entitled is other millennials who don't feel entitled. They get so upset with other millennials that don't show up on time and all those entitled things. They're just like 'What? Why would you think that's OK?'"

However, Kuhl said the entitled label isn't the most damaging stereotype about this generation: It's the belief they are "job hoppers." She said companies have shown reluctance to train and invest in millennials since they think they'll move on to a new job.

"They think, 'I'm just going to make them figure it out on their own," Kuhl said. "But in reality, millennials are thinking 'I'm looking for intellectual growth. I want to be a contributor here.' They are actually a pretty loyal generation."

Some data suggest otherwise. A 2016 Gallup report on millennials indicated that 21 percent of millennials reported changing jobs within the previous year — more than three times the number of non-millennials. The report also said the majority of millennials weren't engaged with their job or company.

On the personal front, millennials are waiting the longest of any of the grown generations to get married and have their own home. According to a 2016 Pew Research Center study and census data on millennials, 32.1 percent lived with their parents, and 57 percent were married by age 30. In comparison, 90 percent of 30-year-olds lived on their own, and 89 percent had married in 1975.

THEY VOTE LESS OFTEN THAN OTHER GENERATIONS

Millennials consistently have the lowest election turn-out among all generations. According to the U.S. Census Bureau, only 17.1 percent of 18- to-24-year-olds voted in 2014, compared with 59.4 percent of those 65 and older.

Why? Some experts on the generation said one of the most prevalent reasons is that millennials tend to move around — a lot.

At some point in their lives, 51 percent of millennials moved for employment, 46 percent moved for or to find a romantic partner, and 44 percent had moved for family, according to a study of 1,000 people between the ages of 18-35 from the moving company Mayflower.

This constant moving around often means re-registering to vote or requesting absentee ballots. However, the 50 states and thousands of counties have different rules, which can lead to confusion.

Some states also passed legislation that seem to target millennials, said Russell Dalton, a political science professor at University of California, Irvine, and author of the book "The Good Citizen: How a Younger Generation is Reshaping American Politics." This includes forcing people to register in person the first time, shortening registration windows, refusing to accept student ID cards or rejecting certain documents as proof of residency.

"There is a whole set of institutional reforms that if politicians wanted to get young people to vote, they could," Dalton said. "But politicians are happy with the status quo."

Abby Kiesa, youth coordinator and researcher for the Center for Information and Research on Civic Learning and Engagement, said several barriers keep young people from voting. Along with the legislative hurdles, Kiesa said communities don't often reach out.

"We don't do a very good job as a country in integrating and welcoming young people into democratic process," Kiesa said.

Moumita Ahmed, co-founder of the group Millennials for Bernie, agreed. She said she's seen her peers struggle with all the steps involved in the registration process.

"Many of us aren't registered because the current election laws are terrible," Ahmed said. "It is actually really difficult, even when you do register, to process the entire thing."

However, even when states and jurisdictions do make it easy to register and vote, it doesn't necessarily mean millennials will make it to the polls.

Millennials often describe themselves as disillusioned and distrustful of the political system. Ryan Keating, a 33-year-old self-described drug policy reform activist from Salt Lake City, said the political system makes millennials feel like they are being talked at, not to. And no one is trying to fix millennial issues.

"Why would millennials be trustful of this system?" Keating said. "It would be hard to come up with the reasons."

According to a 2016 poll by the Harvard University Institute of Politics, 47 percent of millennials feel that America is heading on the wrong track, and 48 percent agree that "politics today are no longer able to meet the challenges our country is facing."

Millennials also lack faith in the traditional two-party system, which is why so many are independent.

"I have no party loyalty to the Democrats – zero," Keating said. "I wish I had a party I could identify with."

Political strategist Luke Macias, CEO of Macias Strategies LLC, said millennials just aren't as connected to local governments as older generations, so they don't see the value in voting.

"There is a level of apathy in millennials, but the baby boomers were apathetic at 18 too," Macias said. "I don't think most millennials see the impact an elected official has on their lives, and as they get older and get more involved, they'll see that these elected officials are the ones making the decisions."

THEY CARE ABOUT A WIDE RANGE OF ISSUES

Because millennials tend to distrust politicians, they often pay more attention and spend their time on issues rather than parties. Maurice Forbes, the youth vote director for NextGen Climate in Nevada, said he sees this trend with college students.

"I hear a lot from theses campuses across Nevada that 'I care about these specific issues that are going to be affecting me and less so about a particular candidate that is expressing their views on that,'" Forbes said.

But it's not just two or three main issues that stand out to millennials. They feel passionate about a wide range of issues.

Millennials don't necessarily consume news and information the same way previous generations did – from the nightly broadcast news or the daily newspaper. But that doesn't mean millennials don't care about the world, according to a study by the Media Insight Project.

In fact, the study suggested that millennials' access to technology and social-media platforms has actually widened their awareness of issues. "Millennials also appear to be drawn into news that they might otherwise have ignored because peers are recommending and contextualizing it for them on social networks, as well as on more private networks such as group texts and instant messaging," the study said.

Harvard student Kevin Sani, a member of the group that launched the college's 2016 political poll, said this constant access to media actually creates a polarization among millennials because they gravitate toward information and sources they care about.

"Nobody really wants to read news that disagrees with them," Sani said. "We all want news that agrees with us as a confirmation of our own beliefs, so that can further enhance the echo chamber effect."

Recent national polls have indicated millennials often care most about the same issues other generations do: No. 1 being the economy (jobs, minimum wage, paid leave), according to a USA Today/Rock the Vote poll.

Money issues also play a big role in their lives, and college affordability and student debt was the second most popular answer. Other top issues included foreign policy and terrorism, health care, guns and climate change, according to the poll.

Their answers ranged from stopping the Islamic State group and ending the so-called war on drugs to eliminating poverty and providing free education from kindergarten to college.

ORGANIZATIONS GET CREATIVE TO REACH POTENTIAL VOTERS

Millennials for Bernie hosted T-shirt screen printing and dance parties. HeadCount traveled to concerts across the country. Rock the Vote went to Comic-Con. And President Barack Obama played Operation and made friendship bracelets on a video on BuzzFeed.

All in the name of voter registration.

Voting groups across the country are realizing if they want to appeal millennials, they've got to make the process fun.

"In a word, that approach makes perfect sense," Hais said. "Millennials, as a civic generation, are very group oriented and other-directed. In addition, it's simply efficient to try to enlist people in venues where they gather in large numbers."

HeadCount, a New York-based nonprofit organization, hosts voter registration drives at music festivals and concerts across the country. By combining music and politics, HeadCount has registered more than 300,000 voters since 2004.

"We're catching people where they're having fun," said Aaron Ghitelman, the communications manager for HeadCount. "If somebody's in a good mood, they're more likely to register."

THEY CAN CHANGE AMERICAN POLITICS

Historically, millennials have not shown up to vote. But that does not mean the generation hasn't influenced political institutions.

The millennial population overtook baby boomers as the largest generation in 2015, according to the U.S. Census Bureau. In Utah, the millennial generation has been larger since at least 2000, according to the Utah Foundation, a public policy research firm.

Salt Lake City is home to the second-highest percentage of 25- to 34-year-olds in the country among major cities – second only to Austin, Texas. And the city's politics reflect its young population.

The city has long been a left-leaning island in the middle of historically conservative Utah, but the city's politics are becoming even more progressive – and

"The old, white baby boomers get old, leave the labor force, eventually die and then, the young generations – which are so profoundly multicultural, multilingual, multiethnic and just have completely different life experiences and sensibilities than baby boomers – are becoming the majority population just through the advance of aging," Perlich said. "We're going through a time of really terrific change, really unprecedented."

Hais predicts that when millennials begin to take office, the hyper-partisan nature of politics will shift to something more compromise driven.

"What we will see is a change in the way things are done politically," Hais said. "What we see now is terrible gridlock because of that baby boomer division. They can't see eye to eye, but millennials will be different. Millennial Democrats and millennial Republicans are closer together."

1. Despite not voting, the authors feel millennials are still changing politics. How, and what could these trends mean for the future of politics?

2. How has student debt impacted the way millennials engage with politics?

"MILLENNIALS REJECT CAPITALISM IN NAME – BUT SOCIALISM IN FACT," BY BK MARCUS, FROM THE FOUNDATION FOR ECONOMIC FREEDOM, MAY 23, 2016

"In an apparent rejection of the basic principles of the US economy," writes Max Ehrenfreund at the *Washington Post*, "a new poll shows that most young people do not support capitalism."

Notice the intimation that capitalism is the system we already have — not, as pro-capitalist philosopher Ayn Rand called it, the "unknown ideal." But Ehrenfreund takes a half step back from the implication: "Capitalism can mean different things to different people." Nevertheless, he concludes, "the newest generation of voters is frustrated with the status quo, broadly speaking."

So we're not entirely sure what "capitalism" means to those surveyed, but we think it has something to do with the system we currently live in. Young dissatisfaction with the status quo is probably a good thing, but the labels used in simplistic survey questions — and in headlines — just add ever more confusion to discussions of economic freedom.

As I wrote about my anti-capitalistic youth in "Why Students Give Capitalism an F,"

> "Capitalism" was just the word we all used for whatever we didn't like about the status quo, especially whatever struck us as promoting inequality. I had friends propose to me that we should consider the C-word a catchall for racism, patriarchy, and crony corporatism. If that's what capitalism means, how could anyone be *for* it?

But even advocates of economic freedom are divided on the word *capitalism*. Some see it as the correct name for the system we support, including individual liberty, private property, and peaceful exchange. Of particular significance to Austrian economist Ludwig von Mises, the term "refers to the most characteristic feature of the system, its main eminence, viz., the role the notion of capital plays in its conduct" (*Human Action*, chapter 13).

In other words, the profound abundance that the market has produced for all of us is the result of private investment and economic calculation.

Others point out that the term was coined by the enemies of the free market, and that it has too long a history as the designation for cozy business-government partnerships and legal privilege for the rich and powerful. (See FEE contributor Steven Horwitz's "Is the Name 'Capitalism' Worth Keeping?")

Both sides seem to agree, however, that the word has too many divergent connotations to be used usefully without explanation. Unfortunately, that means we have to spend a lot of time explaining what we don't support.

Zach Lustbader, a Harvard senior involved in conducting the recent poll, told the *Post*, "You don't hear people on the right defending their economic policies using that word anymore." When they do use the word, it is to stand against "crony capitalism," according to the 22-year-old student.

I wish, in his discussion of the problems with the word *capitalism*, Lustbader hadn't fallen back on the even more problematic classification of *people on the right*, but if we put aside that quibble, I can say that his experience matches my own. When I encounter the words *capitalist* or *capitalism* used without qualification, it is most often by those who oppose the free market — and assume an audience that shares that bias.

Other polls of 18-to-29-year-olds show not just antipathy to the word *capitalism* but also generally positive feelings about the word *socialism*. But the results tell us more about semantic reflexes than they do about specific positions on economic policy.

In the Harvard poll, only 27 percent said the government should play a substantial role in regulating the economy. Doesn't that imply that 73 percent support relative economic freedom, no matter what terminology the respondents embrace? Even if millennials don't reject *socialism* as a dirty word, just 30 percent believe in a large government role in reducing income inequality. Even Keynesianism, stripped of its label, fails to garner support: a mere 26 percent think government spending can effectively increase economic growth.

"It is an open question," Ehrenfreund writes, "whether young people's attitudes on socialism and capitalism show that they are rejecting free markets as a matter of principle or whether those views are simply an expression of broader frustrations with an economy in which household incomes have been declining for 15 years."

So we're back to the idea that *capitalism* stands for whatever people perceive to be wrong with the economic status quo. That leaves us with the considerable task of explaining how government interventions, not free markets, got us into the current mess, and how only greater economic freedom can get us out.

But we can take heart from poll results that reveal skepticism toward greater government involvement in the economy: between two thirds and three fourths are dubious of the government's ability to fix anything. That's a start.

1. Do you agree that millennials seem to not understand what capitalism is? Or do you think this is an easy tactic used by the author to further his point?

2. According to this article, just 30 percent of millennials believe that the federal government can help reduce income inequality. What do you think?

CHAPTER 3

MILLENNIALS AND ACTIVISM

Although many millennials are unsure of politics, they care deeply about social justice and equality. Critics of the generation have called them narcissistic, but that's far from true. For many millennials, activism and advocacy are of the utmost importance, and that shows in how they use social media as a platform to promote change and in the issues about which they drive the conversation. From race to the environment, millennials are at the forefront of progress. In this chapter, we'll hear from nonprofit leaders and experts about how millennials are using their focus on social justice to make the United States a more equal place, and what millennial leadership could mean for the country.

"BLAME PARENTS FOR MILLENNIALS' LAUGHABLE FRAGILITY," BY DAVID FRENCH, FROM THE *NATIONAL REVIEW*, MAY 14, 2016

It's hard to doubt that legendarily entitled Millennial social-justice warriors will finally go too far, and not even The Onion will be able to sufficiently parody their aggressive fragility. In a campus culture saturated with controversy over trigger warnings and so-called micro-aggressions, my favorite story comes from Brown University.

Even some of Brown's coddling administrators had to shake their heads at the student response to a debate between leftist feminist Jessica Valenti and libertarian Wendy McElroy. A campus debate is usually a tame-enough event, but this debate would deal with the alleged campus-rape crisis, and McElroy was expected to depart from college orthodoxy and dissent from the myth that women at American universities are uniquely in danger of being raped.

To help students "recuperate" from the debate, student activists set up a "safe space" that featured coloring books, cookies, Play-Doh, and videos of puppies. Yes, adult students at one of the world's most prestigious universities intentionally re-created a day-care center for one another.

Conservatives often alternate between laughing at Millennials' fragility and expressing alarm at its long-term consequences. Viral videos show the campus meltdowns in living color and students so eager to demonstrate their tolerance that they can't bring themselves (in one famous example) to say a five-foot-nine white man is "wrong" to self-identify as a six-foot-five Chinese woman.

Yet in attacking Millennial activists and their administrative enablers, we not only mislabel their malady — they're not nearly as fragile as they claim — we also fail to identify the real culprits. Snowflakes aren't spontaneously generated. They're made, formed largely by parents who've loved their children into the messes they've become.

The upper-middle-class American style of parenting is creating a generation of children who are trained from birth to believe three things: first, that the central goals of life are success and emotional well-being; second, that the child's definitions of success and emotional well-being are authoritative; and third, that parents and other authority figures exist to facilitate the child's desires. If the child is the star of his own life's story, then parents and teachers act as agents, lawyers, and life coaches. They are the child's chief enablers.

Parents, for their part, didn't set out to raise fragile children. Instead, they desperately desired that their kids first be safe and happy. Then — later — safe, happy, and successful. Faced with kids they loved and perhaps still reeling from their own childhood problems, including growing up during the first massive wave of divorce and in an era of increasing crime, Millennials' parents (younger Boomers and older members of Generation X) decided that they were going to get parenting right.

The superficial displays of their parental care and caution are there for all to see. Out of exaggerated fear for their children's physical safety, upper-middle-class mothers and fathers devote themselves to "helicopter parenting," hovering and doing all they can to smooth the bumps of life, well into their offspring's young-adult years.

Why are such fragile, fearful children simultaneously so aggressive? New York University social psychologist Jonathan Haidt has dubbed this phenomenon the "flight to safety" and sees its manifestations in parents who "pulled in the reins" to keep their children from roaming as freely as kids in generations past. Playgrounds were redesigned. Schools put in place "zero tolerance" policies to squelch even the hint of violence. The message was simple: Even in a time of declining crime and exploding prosperity (especially for upper-income families), the world was dangerous and full of terrors.

But why are such fragile, fearful children simultaneously so aggressive? Isn't such strident activism inconsistent with the fear hypothesis? Haidt ascribes much of their ideological aggression to having grown up in an age of increasing polarization. Simply put, Republicans and Democrats hate one another more than ever. Writing in *The Atlantic*, Haidt and Foundation for Individual Rights in Education president Greg Lukianoff note that "implicit or unconscious biases are now at least as strong across political parties as they are across races." Thus, "it's not hard to imagine why students arriving on campus today might be more desirous of protection and more hostile toward ideological opponents than in generations past."

This analysis rings true but seems incomplete. In addition, a lifetime of experience has told student activists that complaints to parents and teachers get results. Thus, the paradox of the modern Millennial snowflake. In the name of their own alleged vulnerability and fragility, they engage in dramatic protest, seek conflict, and relentlessly attack opponents. These snowflakes are dangerous.

How does this happen? Think of the dilemmas that parents face because of their children. Their children participate in sports and run into a coach who is perceived as too angry or who doesn't give the child a fair chance. They go to school and inevitably encounter teachers who don't teach well or who teach subjects they find irritating or challenging. On the playgrounds, they face their first bully or their first physical conflict. And at each stage, they do what kids do: They tell their parents.

When I went to my parents with these dilemmas, the response was often some form of "Suck it up." I once told my dad that my coach threw a basketball at a kid's head when he was talking during practice. My dad laughed. When I broke my right arm in fifth grade, I asked if I could get a break on homework while I learned to write with my left. My dad told me the struggle would teach me how to work hard. If parents ever intervened in playground conflicts, the shame was deep and enduring.

These are small but telling examples from life's little challenges. My parents' priority was building character, not maintaining my happiness. They wanted to raise a child who would love God and live by the Golden Rule. So I had to learn that I wasn't the center of the universe. I had to learn that I was often wrong. And I had to learn the daily courage necessary to confront and overcome problems on my own, without constantly appealing to a higher earthly authority for aid and comfort. We mislabel them as fragile because their unhappiness comes so easily and their tolerance for adversity is so low.

Presently, however, many parents view their child's pain, anger, or inconvenience less as an opportunity to teach the child a lesson about character and perseverance than as an imperative to come to the child's rescue. Thus, parents themselves confront the angry coach, find all the help the child needs to succeed academically (including sometimes even doing homework for the child), talk to the principal about playground conflict, and negotiate with teachers to optimize the child's classroom experience.

The parent emerges first as savior, then as friend. All decent parents covet a relationship with their child, but there are countless times when parent and child naturally clash, and — especially as those children get older — the clashes can strain or fracture the relationship. Parents preserve friendships with their kids in countless small ways: extending curfews on request, purchasing items that strain the family budget, excusing minor infractions of family rules. If the choice is between confront and consent, parents consent again and again, each time vowing to themselves that they'll stand up to their child if the issue is "truly" big.

Not long ago, I was speaking to the headmaster of a large Christian school who was lamenting the extraordinary power children exercised in the parent–child relationship. In the aftermath of the *Obergefell* decision, the school was considering changing its policy handbook to clearly state that the school teaches that marriage is the union of a man and a woman. The headmaster said that he'd already received pushback from parents, not because the parents had any real conviction on the issue (and those who did were generally quite conservative) but because *their children* demanded the parents take a stand. The definition of marriage had become a strain in the parent–child relationship, and parents deferred to their children to remain "friends."

Stories like this are legion. Impose virtually any limit on a child's desires and there is sure to be a parental revolt that begins with the phrase, "My child wants . . . " The rest of the argument flows entirely from the child's desire, which overrules all other reasoning.

We mislabel them as fragile because their unhappiness comes so easily and their tolerance for adversity is so low. But they are not weak. They're instead doing exactly what they've been taught to do since that first bad soccer practice or kindergarten conflict. They scream as loudly as they can for Mom and Dad — for the teacher or the principal, acting in loco parentis — and the authority figure duly obeys. And why not? When happiness and friendship are the goals, when comfort is the highest calling, the response will be immediate. If it's not, then kids will find new friends.

Graduation season is upon us. At countless dinners, emotional parents and children will reflect on their journey, and two sentences will be uttered time and again: "Mom, you weren't just my mother. You were also my best friend." Those words, tearfully delivered and gladly received, are the reason that the present cultural trend is likely to endure, at least for the foreseeable future. Parents are raising exactly the children they want to raise.

But it cannot last. Life is too hard, and authority figures are ultimately too weak to guarantee enduring joy and success. So the aggressively fragile generation will face a choice: either greater anger and aggression as they desperately flail for the utopia that can never come, or a rediscovery of the virtues that enable perseverance. Life is too hard, and authority figures are ultimately too weak to guarantee enduring joy and success.

In the Bernie Sanders phenomenon, we see the flailing. Out from under their parents' roof, out from under the watchful eye of sympathetic administrators, who's the parent now? Who has the authority to address their grievances and ease their fears? Responding to the fear and uncertainty, a geriatric socialist (a fatherly sort of fellow) steps in with his call for free health care and education (neither in fact free), and protection from the rough-and-tumble world of liberty and markets. In other words, Sanders wants to make the entire country a "safe space."

College campuses are centers of Sanders support in large part because they represent small examples of the world he wants to build. Tuition represents an extreme form of progressive taxation as rich families fund generous breaks for the poor, and everyone enjoys the same, often luxurious facilities. Each student has access to an immense social-welfare infrastructure, complete with diversity offices for every ethnicity and easy access to doctors and counselors. College is the ultimate nanny, and many former students miss her warm embrace.

It's a popular sport to scorn entitled Millennials — I'm guilty of it myself — but when people live as Millennials were raised to live, where does the lion's share of the blame lie? Parents placed their child's joy first in large part because it made them happy. It seemed win-win. Parents and children enriched each other's lives as parents fed off the joy they provided their kids. Life as an adult is not a problem so easily solved. Eventually children leave home (and Brown and Yale), and when they do, they find that temper tantrums are not so well received, authority figures don't prioritize their joy, and the hard work of building character must be started now, years late. Even Bernie Sanders cannot heal the hurt to come.

1. Do you agree that millennials are overly "fragile"? Why or why not?

2. So-called "helicopter parenting" has been in the news in recent years. Do you think such a parenting style could harm future generations? Why or why not?

"HOW THE DIGITAL AGE CHANGED YOUTH ACTIVISM," BY FRANK DUTAN AND CARSON MCGRATH, FROM *THE GROUNDTRUTH PROJECT*, JULY 21, 2016

The millennial generation is the largest and most diverse generation in US history.

And according to the Pew Research Center, millennials now have the numbers to outvote any other generation before them, including the biggest voting age group, the Baby Boomers.

Yet millennials' voter turnout rates are significantly lower than those of other generations, ranging from 46 to 50 percent during the last three presidential elections.

Illinois state Rep. Will Guzzardi said millennials are restless and tired of a gridlocked Congress that cannot cooperate. Political polarization halted legislation on the issues millennials are most concerned about — which are education, healthcare and the economy, according to a Millennial Impact Report released last month with support from The Case Foundation.

Down the same streets in Washington, D.C., protesters in the 1960s stormed to voice their opposition to the racial, social and environmental injustices of the time. Millennials today are not only getting involved in government, but are marching with signs, singing chants, and holding their fists in the air in defiance of the same injustices their parents and grandparents fought to abolish.

"[It was] a coalition effort of more than 300 groups working to bring thousands of people to Washington in support of money out of politics and voting rights reforms – which is the first time those issues have been put together on this level, so it is a historic action," said Elise Orlick, a democracy fellow with U.S. PIRG.

Though millennials now have power in numbers, they still represent a minority of people in government. This is where organizations like MAP and the Future Caucus come in. Events like DA allow for millennials to physically air their grievances so that their peers in office can listen and push for the proper legislation.

Ohio Future Caucus member Frank LaRose said that because many caucus members are new in government, they offer a fresh view of what issues need to be addressed for the long term.

The Republican state senator worked with legislators to create an online voter registration form, making the process more accessible. LaRose said the voice of early-career colleagues helped the online registration come to be.

MAP specializes in engaging millennials in politics through their leadership programs, making it easier to be involved in the political process. MAP focuses on an issue-based approach to politics, rather than a partisan one.

"We do a better job of governing when we consider the opinion of our colleagues across the aisle," LaRose said.

Whereas MAP focuses on political engagement, another organization, founded by millennial Ben Brown and a former energy consultant, lobbies government bodies and negotiates benefits on behalf of America's 80 million millennials.

The Association of Young Americans (AYA) is a member-based organization and, like MAP, is nonpartisan. The organization, founded in May, has a few hundred paying members and is still counting.

"It is our right to communicate with our representatives all the time, and that is where our power comes from," he said.

The organization plans to create engagement platforms that enable young people to contact their elected representatives on all levels – through emails, tweets, and phone calls – on a range of issues. Brown said that he eventually plans to equip members with their own personal lobbying tools.

Political groups like MAP and AYA lay the foundations for connecting young people within government for political action and engagement, and they've created a network of millennial leaders focused on issues that attract young people.

Organizations like Black Lives Matter (BLM), founded by a group of young activists, target racial injustices within the United States.

DeRay Mckesson, a 31-year-old prominent BLM activist, was recently arrested while protesting the police killing of Alton Sterling, an African American male. On July 13, Mckesson and other BLM activists went to the

White House to meet with President Barack Obama to discuss policing and criminal justice.

BLM has currently branched off into many different directions. Mckesson and his comrades have their own organization called WeTheProtesters. They've launched several police and criminal justice reform campaigns, all of which can be found under Campaign Zero, which is a 10-point plan for stopping police violence that was launched earlier this month.

Though the Future Caucus is not formally partnered with BLM, Guzzardi said members understand the effectiveness of working with other groups.

"In order to heal communities, particularly communities of color, but to heal communities all around our state, we have to come together and change the way the system works," Guzzardi said.

This means crossing partisan lines in ways that the Future Caucus, MAP and AYA are doing it. They are leading by example – overcoming differences to lay out long-term solutions that will better this future generation.

This sense of urgency — of foregoing ideological differences to reform our government — was the reason that many millennials took part in Democracy Awakening.

Young people created a hashtag "#StayWoke" to describe their movement and to demonstrate that they are in fact aware of the tumultuous consequences that is to come if congress does not act in time.

Mckesson wore that same phrase on his chest during his arrest in Baton Rouge this month.

Each generation has its activists and politicians, from the Civil Rights Movement to Black Lives Matter, but millennials are the first to walk with smartphones in their pockets. These digital natives have the ability to fuse their virtual and actual realities – hence the viral spread of #staywoke on all social media platforms.

Phillip Duarte, a student-activist at the University of Massachusetts Amherst, opted out of the demonstrations at Democracy Awakening and lobbied Congress instead.

"Yes, it is important that people stay engaged through social media and build power through it," Duarte said. "But then that power needs to translate into actual people getting out onto the streets, going into state houses and Capitol Hill and meeting with their legislators, telling them what they want."

Many millennials feel that the government is not representing their concerns, but by using different methods such as lobbying, protesting and collaborating through post-partisan relationships, they will make sure that their voices are heard.

Groups like MAP, AYA and Democracy Awakening bridge the gap between activism, advocacy and political engagement.

Leaders like Fukumoto predict that this year's presidential election will be a turning point for US politics.

"I do think this presidential cycle is going to call into question the whole way parties operate in the country," she said. "And maybe that's what starts the conversation of, 'We can do this differently.'"

1. What role does social media play in activism among millennials?

2. What characteristics do millennial activist groups share? How are they different from activist movements in the past?

"MILLENNIALS: SAVING THE WORLD ALSO MEANS RUNNING FOR OFFICE," BY MARK K. UPDEGROVE, FROM *THE CATALYST*, SUMMER 2016

The memory still burns bright. During the spring of 1979, in my junior year of high school, I ventured by bus with a group of my classmates from suburban Philadelphia to Washington, D.C., for a whirlwind three-day visit that included the standard sites and stops reflecting the splendor of the most powerful country in the world. But the highlight of the trip — not just for me, but for many of my peers — was meeting Peter Kostmayer, the dynamic 31-year old freshman congressman from our district, who spoke to us about the pressing issues of the day. "*A member of Congress—and he's meeting with us!*" we thought.

Since that heady occasion, I've had the privilege of meeting seven U.S. presidents, five of whom I've interviewed on multiple occasions. But I remember distinctly what a big deal it felt like as a 17-year old to meet our congressman in the nation's capital.

To say the least, many millennials don't share my generation's esteem for elected officials. A 2015 Harvard Institute of Politics poll found that a majority of millennials say they would choose to recall all members of Congress if it were possible. A Harvard poll earlier this year revealed that 50 percent of young Americans agree with the statement, "The politics of today are no longer able to meet with challenges our country is facing."

I accept that. Frankly, there's a lot to be cynical about: intractable bi-partisanship breeding incivility and legislative impotence; members of both parties who put politics over country, and ideology over pragmatic compromise; vitriolic, divisive rhetoric clamoring in the media and strewn about social media.

And, after all, disdain for elected officials is nothing new. As Mark Twain wrote in the latter part of the 18th century, "Suppose you were an idiot. And suppose you were a member of Congress. But I repeat myself." That has been bread and butter for everyone from Will Rogers and Johnny Carson to Jon Stewart and Samantha Bee. In many ways, it's healthy.

But what I find troubling is that the millennial generation, which spans the ages of 18 to 34, is generally repelled not only by the political landscape but by the notion of getting involved in politics — directly or indirectly. Jennifer Lawless, an American University professor and author of *Running From Office: Why Young Americans are Turned Off to Politics*, says, "Young people are interested in saving the world and care about making their communities a better place. But they don't consider electoral politics a way to achieve those goals."

While millennials are as involved in their communities as previous generations, volunteering at higher rates, they "see non-profit organizations as more effective and trustworthy than politics and government," according to the book, *Millennial Makeover: MySpace, YouTube, and the Future of American Politics*, by Morley Winograd and Michael Hais.

That generational shift concerns me. There was a time when young people who wanted to make a difference to their country threw their hats in the ring almost instinctively. Young, ambitious members of the World War II generation like John Kennedy, Lyndon Johnson, Richard Nixon, Gerald Ford, and George H.W. Bush ran for and got elected to Congress at ages 29, 29, 33, 35, and 43 respectively.

They saw public service as the best route to making a positive contribution toward America's betterment. So did members of the baby boomer generation: Bill Clinton was governor of Arkansas at 32, George W. Bush ran unsuccessfully for Congress at the same age, and Barack Obama became an Illinois state senator at 35. Even people like Tom Hayden, who railed against the government in the 1960s as a strident Vietnam War protester and member of the "Chicago Seven," later became a California state legislator and senator.

As my wife often says, "Nothing's going to change until something changes." To accept politics as usual is to condone it. In this election season, which clearly signals that Americans are fed up, I hope that younger voters especially will see the changing tide as an opportunity to make their voices heard — not only by casting their ballots, but by having their own names among the candidates on them.

Our government works best when we're all engaged and represented. The ideas and convictions of millennials, who recently overtook baby boomers as the nation's largest living generation, should resound — and they will most resonate if members of their generation get in the game.

To borrow from Mark Twain: Suppose you were a defeatist. And suppose you didn't have faith in your government's effectiveness and credibility but refused to get involved in the process. But I repeat myself.

1. Why is the author concerned that millennials are not running for office? How is this different from past generations?

2. Why might millennials be hesitant to run for public office? What does the author think is the reason they are not seeking election?

"RETHINKING THE MILLENNIAL GENERATION: WHY MILLENNIALS ARE THE FUTURE OF PHILANTHROPY, SOCIAL JUSTICE, AND THE WORKFORCE," BY ROY Y. CHAN, FROM *PHILANTHROPY FOR AMERICA*, JUNE 24, 2016

In the United States, roughly 75 million millennials were born between 1980 and 1997 (U.S. Census Bureau, 2016). As the largest living generation in U.S. history, millennials are expected to make up 50 percent of the workforce by 2020 and 75 percent of the global workforce by 2025 (ProInspire, 2015). Today, the ways that millennials think about social justice issues, their careers, and their giving will have huge impacts on local, regional, and national communities for decades to come. They are already changing and reimagining how nonprofits and philanthropic foundations recruit and retain employees, engage volunteers, and support donors. At the same time, millennials are the most highly educated and tech-savvy generation in U.S. history. They embrace new mobile technology and social media, and are more flexible with career decisions throughout their 20s- and 30s-. Despite the fact that millennials are more educated than any preceding generation of young adults, a recent study from Gallup (2016) found that less than 40 percent of millennials are "thriving" in their professional careers. Furthermore, the Gallup (2016) report suggests that less than 30 percent of employed millennials are engaged at work and that three in 10 young adults do not identify with a particular religion. But why does this all matter for the millennial generation? Why should we care?

As a millennial myself, I often get asked about the key traits that define the largest and most diverse generation in American history: *Are millennials really that different? Are they the most "self-entitled" and "narcissistic" generation in U.S. history?* The answer, quite surprisingly, is both yes and no. While digital and social media may portray the millennial generation as perhaps lazy and self-centered, I have come to discover through my own nonprofit work, Philanthropy for America (PFA), that the two most defining characteristics that define the millennial generation are perseverance and passion. Specifically, through my work with college students and young adults across the U.S., I have discovered that millennials are the most active group with philanthropy and social justice issues than any other previous generations in U.S. history.

Generally, the word philanthropy can be defined by its Greek origin, the "love of mankind." American historian and educator Robert H. Bremmer (1988) defined philanthropy as the "voluntary action for the public good" performed by philanthropists and the wealthy. More specifically, he believed that the aim and function of philanthropy is to improve the quality of human life through education and skills acquisition, climate change, health care, religion, arts/cultures, human resources, etc. Today, the practice of philanthropy occurs in all communities regardless of race, ethnicity, and socioeconomic status. Notably, the role of donors as an external force in American society are reshaping economic and social mobility, education and politics, and intellectual and human life. These gifts and voluntary actions, in turn, have allowed American citizens to pursue social justice issues in the workplace such as, supporting early childhood education programs, combating human trafficking and slavery, eradicating extreme poverty and hunger, promoting criminal justice reform, advancing environmental justice, among others.

Statistically speaking, U.S. donors from individuals, estates, foundations and corporations gave an estimated $373.25 billion in 2015, a 4.1 percent increase over 2014 (Giving USA Foundation, 2016). Of the $373.25 billion, individual giving made up $264.58 billion in which 60 percent of millennials give an average of $481 (Blackbaud, 2013). Furthermore, 84 percent of more than 2,500 millennials surveyed gave to at least one nonprofit organizations, nearly 70 percent of millennials are willing to raise money on behalf of a nonprofit they care about, and more than 70 percent spent at least an hour volunteering in 2014 (Case Foundation, 2015). In other words, American young donors are motivated by passion, purpose, and a drive to change the world. They tend to give and volunteer more frequently, in small amounts, to more causes and charities, and are more likely to help companies/organizations develop future products and services in American society (Kuhl, 2014).

Reflecting back upon my current work PFA, I have learned that millennials have a strong desire to act justly and merciful; to live a long and healthy life; and to remain financially stable. In addition, most millennials I have worked with seek to feel connected and fulfilled with their work; to seek for greater freedom and impact; and to pursue volunteer for nonprofit organizations that may alter and change the very social fabric of America. As the largest living generation in U.S. history, I believe that we must continue to lead the way in answering the call for public justice by rethinking and reframing our engagement with philanthropy to help people escape from poverty in American society. If millennials continue to struggle in the job market, our economy will continue to struggle. And if we as millennials are not thriving with a sense of purpose and a shared vision of justice, we will continue to struggle in life, affecting how we perform as American citizens and consumers of society.

In short, social justice philanthropy has played an enormous role in fulfilling individuals' career goals and promises, and the vitality of American society. The fight to unleash opportunity for underprivileged and underrepresented groups will continue to rely upon millennials to live radically with wisdom, knowledge, and grace through philanthropy and social justice. The real question is: will you join other millennials in the fight for the physically impoverished people of the world?

1. How does the author feel his generation is impacting philanthropy and social justice?

2. What will the millennial influence mean for non-profits and advocacy in the future?

FROM "HOW MILLENNIALS ARE STEPPING UP TO ADDRESS UN POST 2015 AGENDA THROUGH ENTREPRENEURSHIP AND INNOVATION," BY KAROLINA STAWINSKA, FROM *HUMAN DEVELOPMENT PROJECT*, JULY 7, 2015

We the people. These mark the first three words of the United Nations Charter. With over half the world's population being under 30 today, millennials represent 1.8 billion of our world's human workforce. Fearless, ambitious, and entrepreneurial young minds around the world are leveraging technology to build creative solutions to address some of the world's most pressing challenges. Will they succeed at building a global movement that will revolutionize international development? They certainly are not afraid to dream big.

June 26th, 2015 marked the 70th Anniversary of the signing of the United Nations Charter in San Francisco. To celebrate this historic moment, Blake MacDonald and I invited 50 millennial innovators, youth leaders, and UN officials to gather on the 25th of June at the Fairmont

EARLY DETECTION OF CARDIOVASCULAR DISEASE

Connor Landgraf and Jason Bellet are the co-founders of Eko Devices, an intelligent stethoscope attachment which is often referred to as the Shazam for heartbeats—detecting the slightest murmurs in heartbeats through a simple smartphone application. Cardiovascular disease affects 1 in 4 of the world's population. Their technology has the potential to empower doctors and healthcare providers with a simple diagnostic tool, eliminating the need for expensive technology; thus bringing 21st century healthcare to the developing world. The Eko team recently became the youngest team to ever file clearance with the FDA.

PHYSICAL MOBILITY

Michal Prywata and Tiago Caires, not yet 25 years old, have built the world's first brain controlled prosthetic. As founders of Bionik Labs, they have built a robotic exoskeleton for patients with physical mobility impairments. The device allows patients to rehabilitate and walk with the help of technology. To date they have raised over $12,000,000 to fund further research. Their innovative device is using advanced algorithms and sensing technology to give paralyzed people who were once in a wheelchair the opportunity for rehabilitation.

GLOBAL ACCESS TO VISION CARE

The World Health Organization currently estimates that 517 million people suffer from vision loss, creating severe economic and educational implications on communities. Many children often have trouble seeing the chalkboard. Daxal Desai graduated in 2014 and is the co-founder of Eyecheck, a simple technology which makes eye care mobile and accessible. The smartphone application empowers doctors with the ability to provide accurate prescriptions by taking two pictures with a mobile phone. The venture's goal is to make vision services available to millions of people, allowing them to live happier, more productive lives.

1. How are millennials using entrepreneurship to achieve social change?

2. Millennials make up a large part of the population around the world and have already created change through protest and advocacy. Given what we know about millennials, how might they change not just the United States, but also the world?

CHAPTER 4

MILLENNIALS AND WORK

Millennials have a high debt burden and have seen the fewest gains from the economic recovery following the 2008 global recession. As a result, many have had to work multiple jobs, take unpaid internships, or hold off on making career changes. But millennials are resourceful, and in the past few years this generation has started to change the way we think about work, as well as the relationship between our careers and our personal lives. In this chapter, we'll look at research on what millennials want from their jobs, as well as hear from experts on how this generation engages with the workforce and what they do differently. We'll also explore how the advantages millennials have—such as being educated—could work against them as they move further into their careers.

"WHY YOUNG PEOPLE AREN'T KEEPING UP: FROM THE JONESES TO THE KARDASHIANS," BY PARFAIT ELOUNDOU-ENYEGUE, FROM *THE CONVERSATION*, JUNE 5, 2016

Across the world, the current generation of youth has been remarkably active in mobilizing against inequality. From the Arab Spring and the global Occupy movement to many political campaigns across the world, young people are often at the forefront of the fight. Efforts to explain this strong mobilization often invoke romantic notions of youthful idealism, economic self-interest or better access to online means of mass mobilization.

Yet, it may simply be that inequality has become more severe among younger groups of people than it is among older ones.

In new research on global population and inequality at Cornell University, my colleague Anila Rehman and I show that inequality among the world's youth often exceeds – and need not follow the same trend as – inequality among adults.

It is unclear how long this has been the case. More historical research is needed, but we can still learn something by contrasting the Joneses and the Kardashians – two iconic families that illustrate social competition in the U.S.

A century ago, people only had to "keep up with the Joneses," an expression that evolved from a 1913 comic strip. Competition for social status was straightforward and it followed three simple lines: it was waged against one's immediate neighbors, it was waged over material possessions and, perhaps most importantly, it was waged mostly among adults. Adults could check their neighbors'

111

possessions and easily see who was holding the short end of the material stick. Compared to these simpler times, competition has since extended beyond the local, beyond the material and beyond adulthood.

BEYOND THE LOCAL

Over time, globalization has transported social competition from a local to an international stage. Neighbors are no longer just seen across the fence. At a time of rising internet access – up from just 1 percent in 1995 to about 40 percent today – neighbors are also peered at through the internet or TV screens.

Families across the world now take their consumption cues from a global elite. This creates risk of overstretching inequality within poorer nations as their upper classes hoard local resources in frantic efforts to keep up with global trendsetters.

The Kardashians, who have a large following around the world, and for some perhaps represent the top of the social ladder in the U.S., have come to replace the Joneses as social trendsetters.

Work by sociologist Arland Thornton and colleagues has captured this convergence in aspirations, showing how survey respondents in countries as far apart as Albania, Vietnam and Malawi agree closely on the meaning of what constitutes a good life.

BEYOND THE MATERIAL

As social competition becomes global, its material standards ratchet up. Cornell economist Robert Frank and other social scientists have described this "luxury fever" that has everyone scrambling to keep up with the very rich who are constantly upping the ante.

Yet, as competition over money and trinkets ramps up, it extends beyond the strictly material. Social status is increasingly based on perceptions, labels, influence and social attention. The Joneses, by simple virtue of proximity, could always call their neighbors' bluff if they attempted to spend well beyond their means. This is less possible with the remote fantasies hawked in the media.

With respect to labels, influence and social attention, it is no longer just about a car, but also its make and model. Not just affluence, but influence. Not just upstaging the neighbors, but taking them off the stage and getting them to become followers, rather than competitors for social attention.

Indeed, the Kardashians' invitation to "keep up" is not so much about competing with but instead "following" the family's tribulations. Mere mortals who cannot draw a TV following can always turn to Twitter and Facebook as vehicles for attention. Despite warnings against its superficial or risky nature, internet followship, and the patina of celebrity it confers, has emerged as a modern marker of social status.

Indeed, to appreciate how much social competition has changed, one needs only to see how the role of television, phones and computers has evolved from commodity to social space. Whereas social status was once derived from having a television or computer, it is now more about being on television or being followed on the internet.

BEYOND ADULTHOOD

As a third and subtler trend, social competition has seen its center of gravity slightly slide from adulthood to youth.

The Joneses competed as a unit, with the adult parents in focus and children in the background. This script has almost reversed, with the Kardashian matriarch directing traffic in the background and her children at the forefront.

Part of this may reflect a broad trend in which cultures are becoming more youth-centric. Yet, it may also signal a faster increase in inequality among younger populations compared to adults.

Youth is a time of economic dependency, and thus analyses of inequality focus on families or parents. We tend to assume that the levels and the experience of economic inequality among the young mirrors the overall inequality, but this is not accurate for several demographic reasons.

In simplest terms: affluent people tend to marry other affluent people, wealthier families tend to have fewer children than poorer ones and affluent parents are more able to invest resources in their children's education and economic mobility.

These demographic patterns work to widen inequality among the world's youth, relative to the inequality found among adults. Moreover, these adverse conditions are increasingly found to some degree across the world. As long as these demographic trends persist, they will continue to raise inequality among youth.

Some of these trends fall outside the realm of policy. Strictly speaking, one cannot legislate romantic love or prevent highly educated people from exclusively marrying one another. However, one can create macro-economic circumstances that offer realistic incentives for lower-income parents to trade larger families for smaller and better-educated progeny. Most importantly, one must strengthen public support for children in countries with the most severe mix of economic and demographic inequality.

1. How is social media changing the way millennials think of social status?

2. What does the author believe is the future of inequality among millennials and other young generations? What might inequality mean for millennials as they age?

"INEQUALITY, STUDENT DEBT AND MILLENNIALS," BY NICOLE WOO, FROM *CENTER FOR ECONOMIC AND POLICY RESEARCH*, NOVEMBER 12, 2014

Three hot topics of discussion these days are the millennial generation, student debt and inequality. But how do they relate to each other? A new look at Federal Reserve data sheds light on this interesting question.

Millennials are the most highly-educated generation of young adults in our nation's history, attaining college degrees at record-high rates. Yet despite their greater educational attainment, they appear to have less wealth at this point in the lives than prior generations.

If not for a sharp increase in student debt since 1989, young working- and middle-class Americans would have actually slightly higher net worths than their counterparts had a quarter century ago. This is a surprising finding in an analysis of the Survey of Consumer Finances by my colleagues at the Center for Economic and Policy Research (CEPR).

Let's be clear: most young working Americans have never had much wealth. In 1989, the net worth of the bottom three-fifths of 18- to 34-year-olds averaged only $3,300. But by 2013, their net worth dropped by $11,000, to an average of $7,700 in net debt. A chief factor in this flip in fortunes is that the average educational debt among this group shot up more than eightfold, from $1,900 in 1989 to $16,300 in 2013.

Much of this debt seems to be burdening those who have the fewest resources to pay it off. For the middle quintile of 18- to 34-year-olds, student debt averaged $3,300 in 2013, while their net worth averaged $11,000 (a drop from $14,400 in 1989). Meanwhile, the student debt of the bottom fifth was almost 13 times larger, averaging $42,700, while their average net worth was a negative $35,400.

When you look at how completely differently this is playing out for those at the other end of the wealth spectrum, you can see how student debt is likely exacerbating inequality among millennials. In 2013, the top two-fifths of 18- to 34-year-olds averaged $6,700 in educational debt — just one-sixth of that of the bottom fifth — while enjoying over $200,000 in net worth. In fact, the top 5 percent of 18- to 34-year-olds saw their average net worth rise from $988,700 in 1989 to $1 million in 2013, while the other 95 percent saw their net worths drop.

The CEPR report looks at other age groups as well: retirees, near-retirees and mid-career workers. It shows that most households had less wealth in 2013 than in 2010, and much less than in 1989. And that doesn't even take into account the fact that younger generations are much less likely to have defined-benefit pensions to rely on in retirement.

This analysis draws a picture of an economy where the bulk of the benefits of the economic recovery have been going to those who already have the most wealth. For millennials who aren't lucky enough to be at the top, educational debt seems to be emerging as the largest obstacle to creating wealth. If policymakers wish to address inequality among this generation, it seems that they have no choice but to address their student debt burdens as well.

1. What has student debt meant for millennial wealth?

2. So far the economic recovery has not helped millennials significantly. What could businesses and the government do to help millennials impacted by the recession?

"LABOR 2.0: WHY WE SHOULDN'T FEAR THE 'SHARING ECONOMY' AND THE REINVENTION OF WORK," BY BERNHARD RESCH, FROM *THE CONVERSATION*, SEPTEMBER 4, 2015

Uber suffered a legal blow this week when a California judge granted class action status to a lawsuit claiming the car-hailing service treats its drivers like employees, without providing the necessary benefits.

Up to 160,000 Uber chauffeurs are now eligible to join the case of three drivers demanding the company pay for health insurance and expenses such as mileage. Some say a ruling against the company could doom the business model of the on-demand or "sharing" economy that Uber, Upwork and TaskRabbit represent.

Whatever the outcome, it's unlikely to reverse the most radical reinvention of work since the rise of industrialization – a massive shift toward self-employment typified by on-demand service apps and enabled by technology. That's because it's not a trend driven solely by these tech companies.

Workers themselves, especially millennials, are increasingly unwilling to accept traditional roles as cogs in the corporate machinery being told what to do. Today, 34% of the US workforce freelances, a figure that is estimated to reach 50% by 2020. That's up from the 31% estimated by the Government Accountability Office in a 2006 study.

RISE OF THE GIG-BASED ECONOMY

In place of the traditional notion of long-term employment and the benefits that came with it, app-based platforms have given birth to the gig-based economy, in which workers create a living through a patchwork of contract jobs.

Uber and Lyft connect drivers to riders. TaskRabbit helps someone who wants to remodel a kitchen or fix a broken pipe find a nearby worker with the right skills. Airbnb turns everyone into hotel proprietors, offering their rooms and flats to strangers from anywhere.

Thus far, the industries where this transformation has occurred have been fairly low-skilled, but that's changing. Start-ups Medicast, Axiom and Eden McCallum are now targeting doctors, legal workers and consultants for short-term contract-based work.

A 2013 study estimated that almost half of US jobs are at risk of being replaced by a computer within 15 years, signaling most of us may not have a choice but to accept a more tenuous future.

The economic term referring to this transformation of how goods and services are produced is "platform capitalism," in which an app and the engineering behind it bring together customers in neat novel economic ecosystems, cutting out traditional companies.

But is the rise of the gig economy a bad thing, as Democratic front-runner Hillary Clinton suggested in July when she promised to "crack down on bosses misclassifying workers as contractors"?

While some contend this sweeping change augurs a future of job insecurity, impermanence and inequality, others see it as the culmination of a utopia in which machines will do most of the labor and our workweeks will be short, giving us all more time for leisure and creativity.

My recent research into self-organized work practices suggests the truth lies somewhere in between. Traditional hierarchies provide a certain security, but they also curb creativity. A new economy in which we are increasingly masters of our jobs as well as our lives provides opportunities to work for things that matter to us and invent new forms of collaboration with fluid hierarchies.

SHARING INTO THE ABYSS?

Critics such as essayist Evgeny Morozov or the philosopher Byung-Chul Han highlight the dark side of this "sharing economy."

Instead of a collaborative commons, they envision the commercialization of intimate life. In this view, the likes of Uber and Airbnb are perverting the initial collaborative nature of their business models – car-sharing and couch-surfing – adding a price and transforming them from shared goods into commercial products. The unspoken assumption is that you have the choice between renting and owning, but "renting" will be the default option for the majority.

Idealists take another tack. Part of the on-demand promise is that technology makes it easier to share not only cultural products but also cars, houses, tools or even renewable energy. Add increasing automation to the picture and it invokes a society in which work is no longer the focus. Instead, people spend more of their time in creative and leisurely activities. Less drudge, more time to think.

The "New Work movement," formed by philosopher Frithjof Bergmann in the late 1980s, envisioned such a future, while economist and social theorist Jeremy Rifkin imagines consumers and producers becoming one and the same: prosumers.

FROM SELF-EMPLOYMENT TO SELF-ORGANIZATION

Both of these extremes seem to miss the mark. In my view, the most decisive development underlying this discussion is the need for worker self-organization as the artificial wall between work and life dissolves.

My recent work has involved studying how the relationship between managers and workers has evolved, from traditional structures that are top-down, with employees doing what they're told, to newer ones that boast self-managing teams with managers counseling them or even the complete abolition of formal hierarchies of rank.

While hierarchy guarantees a certain security and offers a lot of stability, its absence frees us to work more creatively and collaboratively. When we're our own boss we bear more responsibility, but also more reward. And as we increasingly self-organize alongside others, people start to experiment in various ways, from peer to peer and open source projects to social entrepreneurship initiatives, bartering circles and new forms of lending.

The toughest tension for workers will be how best to balance private and work-related demands as they are increasingly interwoven.

AVOIDING THE PITFALLS OF PLATFORM CAPITALISM

Another risk is that we will become walled in by the platform capitalism being built by Uber and TaskRabbit but also Google, Amazon and Apple, in which companies control their respective ecosystems. Thus, our livelihoods remain dependent on them, like in the old model, just without the benefits workers have fought for many decades.

In his recent book "Postcapitalism," Paul Mason eloquently puts it like this: "the main contradiction today is between the possibility of free, abundant goods and information; and a system of monopolies, banks and governments trying to keep things private, scarce and commercial."

To avoid this fate, it's essential to create sharing and on-demand platforms that follow a non-market rationale, such as through open source technologies and nonprofit foundations, to avoid profit overriding all other considerations. The development of the operating system Linux and web browser Firefox are examples of the possibility and merits of these models.

BETWEEN HELL AND HEAVEN

Millennials grew up in the midst of the birth of a new human age, with all the world's knowledge at their fingertips. As they take over the workforce, the traditional hierarchies that have long dictated work will continue to crumble.

Socialized into the participatory world of the web, millennials prefer to self-organize in a networked way using readily available communication technology, without bosses dictating goals and deadlines.

But this doesn't mean we'll all be contractors. Frederic Laloux and Gary Hamel have shown in their impressive research that a surprisingly broad range of companies have already acknowledged these realities. Amazon-owned online shoe retailer Zappos, computer game designer Valve and tomato-processor Morning Star, for example, have all abolished permanent managers and handed their responsibilities over to self-managing teams. Without job titles, team members flexibly adapt their roles as needed.

Mastering this new way of working takes us through different networks and identities and requires the capacity to organize oneself and others as well as to adapt to fluid hierarchies.

As such, it may be the fulfillment of Peter Drucker's organizational vision:

> ... in which every man sees himself as a "manager" and accepts for himself the full burden of what is

basically managerial responsibility: responsibility for his own job and work group, for his contribution to the performance and results of the entire organization, and for the social tasks of the work community.

1. How are millennials changing the nature of work? What do these changes mean for the future of careers and jobs?

2. How is technology influencing millennials' approach to work?

"WHY ARE SO FEW MILLENNIALS ENTREPRENEURS?" BY ZACHARY SLAYBACK, FROM THE *FOUNDATION FOR ECONOMIC EDUCATION*, JUNE 20, 2016

[*Editor's note: Links to sources can be found in the original article.*]

There's a popular trope right now that a ton of young people are founders and entrepreneurs. Thanks to a handful of young founders with a disproportionate impact (ala Mark Zuckerberg) and cultural figures like HBO's *Silicon Valley*, you can easily trick yourself into believing that entrepreneurship is all the craze among young people. Hacker meetups, entrepreneurship clubs and majors on college campuses, and the sudden growth of incubators

local government, incorporate as a business, get a federal EIN for tax purposes, buy a regulation-friendly sign, and hire staff at a much higher price than her nephew was willing to do the work. And that's just to get off the ground and get started.

Is it any wonder that Tina doesn't go into business today?

TAXING INVESTMENT

One of the most nefarious taxation schemes to small business and entrepreneurial growth is the capital gains tax. Used in this election cycle to refer to taxes on "hedge fund managers" (a boogeyman of choice in Election 2016), the capital gains tax is, simply put, the tax on gains from investments. This applies to all sorts of investments, not just millions of dollars made from trading in some dark room like in *The Wolf of Wall Street*. If you flip a house, you have to pay a capital gains tax. If you invest in commodities (i.e., oil, gold, silver, sugar, copper), you have to pay a capital gains tax. If you start a business that issues dividends, you have to pay a capital gains tax.

Most investments (including launching a small business) come with a certain level of risk and are only made if the would-be investor can expect a minimal growth on the payout. If they know that half of their profits are going to be taxed away by the feds and the state government, many people will decide to forego the investment in the first place. Why work twice as hard at creating a profitable business so that you can keep just as much (if not less!) than a waged job would provide?

I have a good friend who flipped a house when he was 16 years old. He and a few friends put all the money they had saved up together to buy an old house. With a loan from the bank, they owned the house and renovated it heavily. They ended up selling it for a 3x ROI. By the time the state and federal taxes were through, they each received a few thousand dollars over their initial investment. At that point, *it would have been wiser to go work at McDonald's for a year* rather than work on the house.

People invest less when they know that more of their returns will be taken from them.

If you have to pay an income tax and a capital gains tax on everything that you worked so hard to build as a small businessperson, what incentive remains to start in the first place? Sure, there are stories about being the one in charge of your work and how good that feels, but you have to pay your bills at the end of the day. Young people know this too well after years of little-to-no financial education and then seeing the FICA taxes on their paychecks the first few times.

OCCUPATIONAL LICENSURE AND COST OF WORKING

It's not uncommon to have to pass tests in certain states in order to do your trade. If you're a doctor or an airline pilot, this might make intuitive sense. But what about a florist? Or a hair braider? An interior designer? How about these 102 lower-income occupations?

Defenders of occupational licensure will usually find fringe cases where being "properly qualified" to do a job would have supposedly prevented a negative outcome or will point to how hard they had to work to get to where they are today, but these licenses are almost always just some kind of rent-seeking by firms currently in the market trying to keep out potential competitors. Most of these boards and exams are designed and/or judged by existing firms (would-be competitors) and can be extremely costly.

Going back to our hairdresser, Tina, she would have to pass her state qualifications before she can dress hair for people. If she wanted to do cutting at her shop, there's a good chance she'd have to pass another set of tests and requirements before she can offer that radical service. This means she'll have to find the time to go to classes, the money to pay for classes and offset the cost of not working while taking classes, and hope that she passes the examination at the end of the classes.

She may, then, be forced to join a union and pay union dues on top of everything else. (Consider this case of a woman who wasn't even trying to launch a caretaking business and was forced by the SEIU to join a caretakers' union while caring for her ill son.)

GROWING YOUR BUSINESS

Let's say you're a young person who has decided to bear the brunt of the capital gains tax on top of an income tax, the brunt of the regulations declaring how you can and cannot make your living, and even the brunt of any occupational licensure, now it's time to build your business. After operating for a few months, you realize you could use an extra set of hands around your studio to help organize and clean up. You have a friend who is willing to do it in his spare time for a little gas money on the side.

Not so fast! This gas money doesn't cover the minimum wage that your friend is entitled to by law. If you fail to pay him this and the department of labor finds out, you'll be slapped with fines making business impossible for a firm of your size.

So you decide to pay him a minimum wage. Your margins continue to shrink but you could use the extra hands around. As you grow, you could use a second specialist to join you. You have to cut your friend in order to pay for the specialist. The combined cost wasn't worth the marginal addition in value.

It's time to open a second location. Hooray! You've been impressive in your growth and can reinvest some of your profits into a new location. You'll employ more people, serve more happy customers, and all the while grow as a business.

You want to move into the next county over where there is a larger customer base. You find the property, have an agent hired, and are ready to go when you look into the regulations. This new county requires a number of additional licenses to do business and levies a county tax on "corporations." The voters likely thought this meant some company that has offices all over the world and employs people in suits to eat babies — but it turns out that your business is, too, a corporation. You pull back your plans for expansion and settle on staying in your county.

TECH: A FREE DOMAIN?

Young people are more likely to take a "safe" and "stable" job than own a business, recent data indicate.

The heavy regulations and taxes placed on trade-based and investment-based businesses might explain why more young people are interested in launching tech companies instead of these traditional operations. Government regulators are notoriously slow to figuring out new technologies (I still have to pay my municipal sewage bill by mail) and the decentralized, low-cost nature of the Internet makes it harder to levy regulations on firms based there instead of a brick-and-mortar location. It should be no surprise, then, that this area is more prone to seeing startups than elsewhere. The regulations levied on a digital marketing firm are fewer than those of a traditional ad agency or for a logistics app instead of a taxi service. Software engineering is a totally new trade compared to construction, and the forces at play stifling construction have yet to develop for software engineering.

As government regulators and rent-seekers learn the ropes of Internet-based firms and as their tracking technologies improve, expect to see it become much harder to create a tech-based product and company.

DROWNING IN DEBT

Legal and regulatory barriers to entry likely discourage a good number of would-be entrepreneurs who are lucky enough to get that far in the planning process. Unfortunately, for more and more young Americans, debt from student loans takes a higher priority than entrepreneurial planning.

Increasing costs of college combined with easy-money from government-backed agencies and banks have made it that around 71% of graduates in 2015 had student loans (up from 64% in 2005 and up from < 50% 20 years ago). The average borrower in 2015 has more than

$35,000 in student loan debt. (source) And the trends are just pointing to these numbers increasing.

Launching a risky venture with no guarantee of return on investment is hard enough without debt — it's nearly impossible when you have hundreds of dollars of student loans to pay back every month. Even if you can get the loans deferred, you still have to worry about whether or not you'll get to the income levels needed to pay it off in the future.

The Philadelphia Fed reported a strong negative correlation between business formation for businesses with one to four employees and student loan debt. Similarly, areas with a high amount of student loan debt also see the smallest growth in small businesses.

Most small businesses are funded with personal debt in the form of small loans from banks and acquaintances and credit card debt, not huge venture capital pushes as depicted in recent media. Crushing student loan debt makes it harder to manage a $10,000 line of credit on a credit card or a loan from a bank.

But if we recall the WSJ report showing the decline in business ownership between 1989 and 2015, we'll see that the biggest dip happened before the recent spike in outstanding student debt. The growth in lifetime-crushing student debt likely contributes heavily to the decline in the past 15 years, but the fact that a large dip happened before this period might indicate that the problem isn't that fewer people can't start businesses but rather that people don't want to start businesses.

Young people are more likely to take a "safe" and "stable" job than own a business, recent data indicate. There are a variety of additional factors that influence this, but one of the largest is the level at which young people are schooled. The current generation of recent graduates and young professionals is more schooled than any generation before them. Despite this, a growing skill gap and discontentment with work and personal life plagues them.

OVER-SCHOOLED AND OVER-CODDLED: RISK

The preference of a "safe" and "stable" job (assuming there is such a thing) over owning a business is likely a consequence of being more risk averse than prior generations. Young people today grew up in a weird paradoxical world of being rewarded for everything and being instilled with an intense fear of failure.

Being told that you deserve a reward just for participating creates an odd sense of resentment to even trying in most children. Children are smart enough to know when they are being talked down to, and adults giving them awards for not doing their best feels patronizing, even to a six year old. Why work harder if it is just going to result in the same kind of reward? Why try to get somebody to praise you if they'll do it when you fail anyway?

As children grow older and move into the competitive middle school and high school environments, failure takes on a new tone. Failing at school — which takes up the vast majority of a young adult's life from 6 AM – 5 PM most days for the first 18 years — amounts to failing at much of life. Failing an exam or a class translated into failing out of the top echelon of the schooling world — you wouldn't amount to much in school, wouldn't get into a university of your choice, wouldn't get the job you wanted, and would be relegated to an unhappy existence for the rest of your life. Many, many schoolchildren would rather cheat on exams and risk being caught than risk failing the exam outright.

Even in the extra-curricular world, young adults are overworked and overscheduled. Between competition from peers and pressure from parents, a young person competing in anything from soccer to quiz bowl can't afford to fail. The cost of being found out as a cheater or as a flake are lower than the perceived costs of failure.

A healthy level of risk-tolerance is necessary for success in business. Even traditional businesses have to take risks in taking out loans, trying out new products, and offering services in the community. Most successful entrepreneurs are courageous — a trait that school and a coddling parental generation can beat out of young people.

OVER-SCHOOLED: DEGREE INFLATION

Most business owners held some kind of other job before launching their business. If they're working in the startup world and are offering a new and unique service, chances are even higher that they worked for years in a specialized field before launching their product or service. The spike in degree inflation has made it harder to enter the workforce at a younger age. Jobs that had no or minimal credentialing requirements just a few years ago now require a BA or a graduate degree. It's not uncommon to find internships that require a graduate degree.

Getting your foot in the door and gaining experience as a young person is harder than ever. For many entrepreneurs, this experience at another firm was integral to their own venture. This means that would-be entrepreneurs find themselves putting off ventures for years while they complete the formal education requirements to gain the experience they feel is necessary before launching.

Add in the additional factor of life happening and more would-be entrepreneurs drop from the pool. Having 5 years of experience might have made you 27 before out-of-control degree inflation, but today it very well may make you 33 because you had to spend a few years working internships and getting a graduate degree to get that entry level job. Now you have a wife, a baby, a mortgage, and some debt from school, adding more constraints on the flexibility you need to launch a company. You decide to stay at your old job for your family and keep on your way.

OVER-SCHOOLED: SCHOOLED MINDS

One final factor that I suspect contributes to the decline in entrepreneurship is the effect that schooling has on thinking differently. Successful entrepreneurs (and successful people in general) cite thinking differently than the pack as one of the most important factors for their success. Whether it's making an investment will pay off big time or going to work somewhere that has a lot of potential for growth, these people all set themselves apart first by their thinking that allowed them to make these decisions. They then had the work ethic to carry through and execute on these ideas.

Schools are notorious for promoting conformity of thought and making people resent the idea of working hard. They promote homogeneity of thought through mandatory curricula and separating young people by age. This is no hippie-dippie, new agey bullshit, either. Think about it in terms of economic thinking.

A young person in school has a strong incentive to mold their way of thinking to that of the people around them. In class, they are rewarded for meeting and exceeding expectations on rubrics and standardized tests. Try as they may, it is nearly impossible for teachers to develop a standard curriculum that promotes difference in thought. Smart students know what their teachers want from exams and will give it to them. The cost of doing things differently is much higher than the cost of conforming to standards and expectations. If you do things differently, expect to pay the cost.

In the lunch room and in the halls, little is different. Having different opinions or lifestyle tastes earns a child or young adult the ridicule of peers and the displeasure of being an outcast.

To succeed in the schooling environment requires nearly the exact opposite as succeeding in the marketplace — an above-average work ethic is the only arguable shared trait. Schools reward conformity in thought and problem-solving. They reward conformity in tastes and desires. The kid who wants to go off and do something entirely different than his peers is shunned or at least finds it difficult to make friends. The young adult who solves problems differently than the textbook is slowed down and made to feel inferior. Having a definite focus is discouraged, especially if it does not relate directly to exams. — instead, focus on getting good grades and getting out of school to succeed.

Success as a young entrepreneur requires an element of deschooling — unlearning the bad habits built up during school. In fact, many affluent entrepreneurs *were not high-achieving students in school.*

THE DEVIL'S IN THE INSTITUTIONS

The factors that contribute to whether or not somebody decides to launch a business can be broken down into if they can and if they want to. Increases in taxes and government regulations — especially those on small business owners and tradespeople — combined with an immense spike in student loan debt and stricter lending policies by banks make it harder for those who want to start businesses to even get off the ground. An ever-growing schooling regime that rewards conformity of thought and heavily penalizes risk-taking creates a generation of people who don't even want to become entrepreneurs anyway.

To see the next (and current, lost) generation of business owners, value-creators, and innovators take off, freedom to experiment, fail, and the opportunity to try different things need to be reclaimed.

1. What does the author feel is the reason for the lack of entrepreneurship among millennials? What solutions does he offer?

2. What impact could this trend away from entrepreneurship mean for the economy?

CHAPTER 5

RESEARCH ON MILLENNIALS

Now that we've seen the millennial generation from a few angles, let's look at the research. Although defining an entire generation of millions of people is difficult—if not impossible—researchers have found some trends that can help us sort the fact from the fiction. As the largest generation in the country, the attitudes and values millennials have could shape the country for decades to come. The studies in this chapter are wide ranging, including a look at how millennials compare to past generations and their views as they move into adulthood. We also look at the psychology of millennials, and what work-life balance means to a generation reshaping how we think about careers.

"MILLENNIALS, NEWS AND IMPORTANT TRENDS: RESEARCH DATA FROM THE MEDIA INSIGHT PROJECT," BY JOHN WIHBEY, FROM *JOURNALIST'S RESOURCE*, MARCH 19, 2015

As news organizations prepare for the future, they might be well-served to keep their eyes on an important demographic shift: In 2015, the Millennial generation — those ages 18 to 34, and born between 1981 and 1997 — is set to become larger than the Baby Boom genera-tion. (This will be true, even as the country's median age continues to rise.) Over the next three decades or so, the cohort of Baby Boomers will decline in size steadily, and by mid-century only about 1 in 5 will be living, as the Pew Research Center points out.

As this giant post-war generation — the largest in U.S. history to this point — dwindles, so too will a defined set of news consumption habits that evolved around print newspapers and limited consumer broadcast choice. Meanwhile, a diverse new generation will come to matu-rity with a new set of embedded information, technology and communications practices and values.

A March 2015 report from the American Press Institute and the Associated Press-NORC Center for Public Affairs Research, "How Millennials Get News: Inside the Habits of America's First Digital Generation," draws new insights based on a survey of 1,046 members of the gener-ation, as well as qualitative interviews in select cities. Working together as part of the Media Insight Project, the researchers set out to test some commonly held assump-tions about Millennials — a highly digitally connected cohort — including that they are less interested in news than are past generations. The margin of error for the survey was plus or minus 3.8 percentage points.

The report's findings include:

- Eighty-five percent of Millennials surveyed said keeping up with news is at least somewhat important to them, and 38% said it is "very" or "extremely" important. Forty-five percent said they follow five or more "hard news topics."
- Just under two-thirds (64%) said they regularly follow what's going on in the world and/or consume news articles or broadcasts.
- Among the activities that Millennials engage in online, accessing news ranks somewhere in the middle: "Keeping up with the news falls only slightly behind the three most popular digital activities: checking and sending email (72%), keeping up with what friends are doing (71%), and streaming music, TV, or movies (68%)."
- Among those surveyed, 88% said they get news from Facebook, while 33% said they get news from Twitter. "On 24 separate news and information topics probed, Facebook was the No. 1 gateway to learn about 13 of those, and the second-most cited gateway for seven others."
- Millennials reported encountering a range of opinions among their online information sources, especially those who reported encountering news more casually or incidentally: "Fully 73% of those Millennials who say they mostly bump into news and information throughout their day say the opinions in their feeds are an even mix of viewpoints, compared with 65% of those

who call themselves active news seekers. Bumping into news, in other words, may widen the perspectives one is exposed to, not narrow them."

- There were differences between age cohorts within this generation: "Only a third of the youngest Millennials, those under age 25, describe themselves as mostly pro-active news consumers. By contrast, fully half of those over age 30 do so. These older Millennials are evenly divided between those who mostly seek out news and those who mostly bump into it."

"Millennials consume news and information in strikingly different ways than previous generations, and their paths to discovery are more nuanced and varied than some may have imagined," the report concludes.

1. Why do you think millennials are particularly interested in following the news?

2. How has social media, in your opinion, changed the way millennials interact with the news?

"CREATIVITY AND COGNITIVE SKILLS AMONG MILLENNIALS: THINKING TOO MUCH AND CREATING TOO LITTLE," BY BRICE CORGNET, ANTONIO M. ESPIN, AND ROBERTO HERNÁN-GONZÁLEZ, FROM *FRONTIERS IN PSYCHOLOGY*, OCTOBER 26, 2016

[*Editor's note: Figures and tables are not included here and can be found with the original article.*]

Organizations crucially need the creative talent of millennials but are reluctant to hire them because of their supposed lack of diligence. Recent studies have shown that hiring diligent millennials requires selecting those who score high on the Cognitive Reflection Test (CRT) and thus rely on effortful thinking rather than intuition. A central question is to assess whether the push for recruiting diligent millennials using criteria such as cognitive reflection can ultimately hamper the recruitment of creative workers. To answer this question, we study the relationship between millennials' creativity and their performance on fluid intelligence (Raven) and cognitive reflection (CRT) tests. The good news for recruiters is that we report, in line with previous research, evidence of a positive relationship of fluid intelligence, and to a lesser extent cognitive reflection, with convergent creative thinking. In addition, we observe a positive effect of fluid intelligence on originality and elaboration measures of divergent creative thinking. The bad news for recruiters is the inverted U-shape relationship between cognitive reflection and fluency and flexibility measures of divergent creative thinking. This suggests that thinking too much may hinder important dimensions of creative thinking. Diligent and creative workers may thus be a rare find.

INTRODUCTION

Evidence from a recent survey reports that managers are three times more likely to hire a mature worker than to hire a *millennial* (born between 1980 and 2000; Rainer and Rainer, 2011) despite desperately needing their creative talent.[1] Mature workers are appealing to recruiters because they are seen as more reliable and more committed than millennials. The dilemma for managers is thus to hire millennials that are both diligent and creative. Recent studies have shown that firms can secure the hiring of diligent millennials by relying on measures of cognitive skills. For example, intelligence has been found to be the main predictor of overall work performance in a wide variety of occupations and across age and gender (e.g., Hunter and Hunter, 1984; Olea and Ree, 1994; see Schmidt, 2009 for a review). Standard measures of cognitive ability have been found to correlate positively with task performance (Schmidt et al., 1986; Murphy, 1989) and negatively with counterproductive work behaviors such as theft or absenteeism (Dilchert et al., 2007). Moreover, the results of a recent study suggest that these effects may be mediated by individuals' cognitive styles (Corgnet et al., 2015b). In particular, Corgnet et al. (2015b) find that millennials characterized by a more reflective style (as measured by the Cognitive Reflection Test; Frederick, 2005) are more diligent, displaying higher levels of task performance and lower levels of counterproductive work behaviors.[2] A crucial caveat is whether hiring millennials based on cognitive measures may ultimately select less creative workers. To address this point we need to assess the relationship between cognitive skills and creativity. Traditionally, intelligence, and creativity have been considered to be unrelated (Getzels and Jackson, 1962; Wallach and Kogan, 1965; Batey and Furnham, 2006; Sawyer, 2006; Weisberg, 2006; Runco, 2007; Kaufman, 2009; Kim et al., 2010). In a meta-analysis, Kim (2005) finds that the correlation between creativity test scores and IQ varies widely and is, on average, small (r = 0.174). However, a growing consensus has emerged in recent research stressing a close relationship between intelligence and creative performance (see Silvia, 2015, for a review). This emerging consensus heavily relies on recent studies that have employed more sophisticated statistical techniques and more robust assessment methods than prior research on the topic. For example, the use of latent variable models has allowed researchers to uncover a positive and significant relationship between creativity and intelligence using data from previous studies that reported non-significant correlations (Silvia, 2008b). The recent wave of research on intelligence and creativity has also improved upon traditional assessment of creativity that exclusively relied on scoring methods based on the originality and uniqueness of responses in creative tasks (such as finding unusual uses for an object). These traditional scoring methods are imprecise because they confound several factors, such as fluency and sample size (Hocevar, 1979; Silvia et al., 2008), and can thus lead to inaccurate estimates of the relationship between intelligence and creativity (Silvia,

2008a; Nusbaum and Silvia, 2011). The results of this new wave of research on creativity and intelligence have been taken as evidence that executive cognition is undoubtedly beneficial to creative thinking (Silvia, 2015).

Yet, although there is an obvious link between intelligence and executive cognition, from the point of view of modern dual-process theory (Evans, 2008, 2009; Stanovich, 2009, 2010; Evans and Stanovich, 2013), one should distinguish between algorithmic and reflective cognitive processes. Algorithmic processes are typically associated with computational efficiency and are measured by standard intelligence tests whereas reflective processing is associated with a disposition to employ the resources of the algorithmic mind, that is, to switch from autonomous "Type 1" thought to analytic "Type 2" (working memory-dependent) thought. The reflective mind thus has a disposition-based definition ("cognitive styles", reflective vs. intuitive) and is not adequately measured by standard intelligence tests (which assess "cognitive ability") but by tasks of cognitive reflection like the Cognitive Reflection Test (CRT; Frederick, 2005). Individuals characterized by a more reflective mind tend to show higher levels of self-control and lower levels of "cognitive impulsivity" (Frederick, 2005; Kahneman and Frederick, 2007; Cokely and Kelley, 2009; Oechssler et al., 2009; Toplak et al., 2011; Brañas-Garza et al., 2012).

From this perspective, one can conjecture that cognitive reflection may relate negatively to creativity. This is the case because a number of studies suggest that the capacity to control one's attention and behavior may even be detrimental for creative thinking (for a review, see Wiley and Jarosz, 2012a). For example, creative problem solving has been shown to relate positively to moderate alcohol intoxication (Jarosz et al., 2012), which is known to impair inhibition and attentional control (Peterson et al., 1990; Kovacevic et al., 2012; Marinkovic et al., 2012). Similarly, an "experiential" thinking style (which maps onto Type 1 processing) has been found to correlate positively with creative performance (Norris and Epstein, 2011).

As mentioned, past literature arrived at conflicting conclusions regarding whether executive cognition favors (e.g., Nusbaum and Silvia, 2011; Beaty and Silvia, 2012; Silvia, 2015) or hampers (e.g., Eysenck, 1993; Kim et al., 2007; Ricks et al., 2007; Norris and Epstein, 2011; Jarosz et al., 2012; Wiley and Jarosz, 2012b) creative thinking. Dual-process theory can reconcile these apparently conflicting findings by positing that creativity may be generated by a mix of Type 1 and Type 2 processes (Allen and Thomas, 2011; Ball et al., 2015; Barr et al., 2015; see Sowden et al., 2015, for a review). It follows that the dual-process approach lays out a promising research agenda based on assessing the exact mix of Type 1 and Type 2 processes that bolsters creativity as well as analyzing separately the effect of algorithmic and reflective Type 2 processes on creative thinking.

Following a dual-process approach, Barr et al. (2015) find experimental evidence of an important effect of controlled Type 2 analytic processes on both *convergent* and *divergent* (Guilford, 1967) creative thinking. In particular, they find that both cognitive ability (measured as the combination of numeracy and verbal skills) and reflective cognitive style (average of scores in the CRT and base-rate problem tasks) covary positively with one's capacity to make remote associations, that is, with convergent creative thinking. Regarding divergent creative thinking, Barr et al.

(2015) show that cognitive ability but *not* cognitive reflection predicts higher originality scores in an alternate uses task. Fluency in the latter task, however, was not correlated with either cognitive measure. In this paper, we use a similar approach to Barr et al. (2015) and investigate how both types of cognitive processes affect creativity. In particular, we analyze how cognitive abilities (measured using Raven as a test of fluid intelligence) and cognitive styles (intuitive vs. reflective; as measured by the CRT) relate to convergent and divergent creative thinking. We extend Barr et al. (2015) by analyzing other measures of divergent thinking such as flexibility and elaboration and by exploring possible non-linearities between creativity and cognitive measures.

Given the conflicting results regarding whether executive cognition is beneficial or detrimental for creative thinking, we conjecture that there might exist a non-linear relationship between different measures of creativity and cognition. Specifically, it might be that a minimum level of executive cognition is necessary for creative performance but, beyond some level, the relationship disappears or even turns negative. This might explain why previous findings seem to be inconsistent. A related line of reasoning has been proposed in the socalled "threshold hypothesis" of the relationship between IQ and creativity (Guilford, 1967; Jauk et al., 2013). The threshold hypothesis states that intelligence is positively related to creative thinking for low IQ levels but the relationship blurs for high IQ levels. Similar arguments arise in recent accounts of the "mad genius hypothesis": moderate levels of inhibitory or top-down control dysfunction, characteristic of subclinical psychiatric populations (e.g., mild ADHD and schizophrenia disorders), can spur creativity under some conditions whereas clinical-severe levels typically lead to impoverished creative thinking (Schuldberg, 2005; Abraham et al., 2007; Jaracz et al., 2012; Acar and Sen, 2013; Abraham, 2014).

METHODS

PARTICIPANTS AND GENERAL PROTOCOL

Participants were 150 students (46.67% female; age: mean ± SD = 20.23 ± 1.96) from Chapman University in the U.S. These participants were recruited from a database of more than 2000 students. Invitations to participate in the current study were sent to a random subset of the whole database. This study is part of a larger research program on cognition and economic decision making. The local Institutional Review Board approved of this research. All participants provided written informed consent prior to participating. We conducted a total of 12 sessions, nine had 12 participants and three had 14 participants. On average, sessions lasted for 45 min. All subjects completed the same tasks in the following order: (1) CRT, (2) Raven test, (3) Remote associates task, (4) Alternate uses task. Subjects had 6 min to complete each task and a 2-min break after completing the Raven test.

MEASURES

COGNITIVE ABILITY ASSESSMENT

Participants completed a subset of Raven progressive matrices test (Raven, 1936). Specifically, we used the odd number of the last three series of matrices (Jaeggi et al., 2010; Corgnet et al., 2015a). The number of matrices correctly solved in the Raven test (in our sample, ranging from 9 to 18, mean ± SD = 14.40 ± 2.42 for males and 14.47 ± 2.16 for females) is a conventional measure of cognitive ability. This test captures an important aspect of cognitive processing which is referred to as fluid intelligence and is closely related to algorithmic thinking (Stanovich, 2009, 2010).

COGNITIVE STYLE ASSESSMENT

We measured the participants' tendency to rely on intuition vs. reflection using the CRT introduced by Frederick (2005). The test is characterized by the existence of an incorrect response which automatically comes to mind but has to be overridden in order to find the correct solution. To the original CRT questions, we added four questions recently developed by Toplak et al. (2014). This extended task (see Text S1) will allow us to uncover potentially non-linear relationships that would be hard to observe using the classical three-item task (Frederick, 2005). In Table S1, we display the proportion of subjects answering each question correctly, split by gender. As expected, males performed better in the test than females (Frederick, 2005; Bosch-Domènech et al., 2014). Our measure of cognitive reflection is given by the total number of correct answers (from 0 to 7). The full distribution of correct answers by males (mean ± SD = 4.09 ± 2.31) and females (mean ± SD = 2.89 ± 2.03) is provided in Figure S1.

CONVERGENT CREATIVE THINKING

We used a subset of the Remote Associate Test (RAT; Mednick, 1962) to measure subjects' ability to make remote associations. In particular, subjects were shown 13 sets of three words (e.g., widow-bite-monkey) and asked to find a word which relates to all the three words provided (in this example the solution is "spider"). Our measure of convergent thinking is the number of problems correctly solved (from 0 to 13).

DIVERGENT CREATIVE THINKING

We measured divergent thinking using a variant of the Alternate Uses Task (AUT; Guilford, 1967). Participants were instructed to provide as many unusual uses of a pen as possible during 6 min. We construct four different measures of divergent thinking: *fluency, originality, flexibility, and elaboration.* We measured fluency as the total number of answers provided by a participant. Three raters were presented with a random list of answers and asked to score the degree of originality of each entry using a 1 (*not at all*) to 5 (*very much*) Likert scale. We computed originality as the sum of the average score of the three raters for all the entries provided by a participant, divided by the total number of answers. Following Troyer and Moscovitch (2006) and Gilhooly et al. (2007), all the answers were classified in broad differentiated categories (e.g., uses of the pen as cloth or hair accessories). Then, *flexibility* was measured as the number of different categories provided by each participant. Finally, elaboration refers to the average amount of detail (from 0 to 2) provided by each participant.

STATISTICAL ANALYSIS

For the data analysis, we start by showing the descriptive statistics of all the measures used and their zero-order correlations. To further assess the relationships between creativity and cognitive measures, we first provide a graphical representation using LOWESS smoothing (Cleveland, 1979; Cleveland and McGill, 1985). We then run ordinary least squares regressions which allow us to test the statistical significance of the linear and nonlinear relationships which were shown in the LOWESS graphs. All the analyses were performed using Stata 14.0.

RESULTS

DESCRIPTIVE STATISTICS AND CORRELATIONS

Means, standard deviations, and correlations are shown in **Table 1**. Unsurprisingly, we find moderate positive correlation between the number of correct answers in the CRT and Raven tests ($r = 0.26$, $p < 0.01$) which suggests that CRT and Raven are not entirely measuring the same cognitive skills (Frederick, 2005; Stanovich, 2009, 2010). Similarly, the different measures of divergent thinking (AUT) are significantly correlated (all p's < 0.01), except for *originality* and *flexibility* ($p = 0.28$).

Regarding our cognitive measures, we find that both Raven ($p < 0.01$) and CRT scores ($p = 0.03$) are positively correlated with convergent thinking (RAT). However, the relationship between cognitive skills and divergent thinking is more complicated. High levels of cognitive ability (Raven) relate positively with *originality* ($p = 0.01$) and *elaboration* ($p < 0.01$), but negatively with the number of answers provided (fluency; p = 0.04) and non-correlated with flexibility (p = 0.20). Finally, we do not find a significant correlation between cognitive styles (CRT scores) and any measure of divergent thinking (all p's > 0.26).

NON-LINEAR EFFECTS AND REGRESSION ANALYSIS

We now turn to the study of possible non-linear relationships between our measures of cognition and creativity. **Figure 1** displays all the relationships under study using LOWESS (bandwidth = 0.8; Cleveland, 1979; Cleveland and McGill, 1985). LOWESS is a model-free smoothing technique based on locallyweighted regressions which can detect both linear and nonlinear relationships. In order to compare the effect sizes, we standardize all measures (standard deviations from the mean). We also ran ordinary least squares regressions to assess the statistical significance of the observed relationships. In Tables S2–S6, we present the results of a series of regressions in which we estimated both linear and quadratic effects of each of the predictors (Raven and CRT) separately on each creativity measure (columns [1] to [4]). From these regressions, we selected the models with the best fit, either linear or quadratic in each case, using the Akaike Information Criterion (AIC) and report them in summary **Table 2**. In addition, we ran similar regressions in which both predictors (linear and quadratic terms) are included simultaneously (columns [5] and [6] in Tables S2–S6) in order to test for possible mediation or confounding effects. The interaction between CRT and Raven scores is never significant in predicting creativity (all p's > 0.3) and is thus not reported in the tables for the sake of brevity. The results remain qualitatively similar if we also control for gender and age.

151

The models with the best fit (**Table 2**) report a positive linear relationship of convergent thinking (RAT) with both Raven ($p < 0.01$) and CRT scores ($p = 0.03$), which is consistent with the positive and significant correlations reported in the previous section. Effect sizes are substantial: in both cases, one SD increase in the predictor is associated with about 20% of one SD increase in RAT (0.22 and 0.17 for Raven and CRT, respectively; see coefficients in **Table 2**). Interestingly, the effect of Raven on RAT remains significant ($p = 0.02$) if we include both Raven and CRT scores as predictors (see column [5] in Table S2) whereas the effect of CRT becomes non-significant ($p = 0.15$). This result suggests that the significant effect of CRT scores on convergent thinking is driven more by cognitive ability (basic computational skills are also necessary for solving the CRT correctly) rather than by reflectiveness.

The relationship between our cognitive measures and divergent thinking is more complex. The models with the best fit report a linear and significant relationship between cognitive ability and all the measures of divergent thinking (all p's < 0.03), except for flexibility ($p = 0.22$; see **Table 2**). Subjects with a higher Raven score tend to generate less uses (lower *fluency*), although these are more elaborated and original. Again, for these three creativity measures, one SD increase in Raven produces a variation in the dependent variable of about 20% of one SD. The effect of Raven on *flexibility* appears to be slightly U-shaped in **Figure 1** but the regressions do not report any significant linear or quadratic relationship (all p's > 0.22; see columns [1] and [2] in Table S5). As shown in columns [5] and [6] of Tables S3–S6, the effect of Raven on the divergent thinking measures remains virtually identical when controlling for CRT, which indicates that cognitive reflection does not mediate any of these relationships.

Contrary to the results observed with Raven, we do not find any significant linear relationship between cognitive styles and divergent thinking (all p's > 0.28; see column [3] in Tables S3–S6). These results hold when we control for Raven (all p's > 0.63; see column [5] in Tables S3–S6). However, we find a significant inverted U-shape relationship of CRT with both *fluency* and *flexibility*, as reported in **Table 2** (p < 0.01 and p = 0.02, respectively). Subjects with an average level of cognitive reflection tend to produce more answers and use more categories than those subjects characterized by either a more intuitive or a more reflective cognitive style. Moreover, the fact that the coefficient of the linear term in the quadratic regression specification is not significantly different from zero in either case (p = 0.52 and p = 0.88, respectively) indicates that the maximum levels of fluency and flexibility are observed at the mean CRT score, as suggested by **Figure 1**. Effect sizes are comparable to those reported above insofar as, in both cases, moving one SD either above or below the mean CRT is associated with a decrease of about 20% of one SD in the dependent variable. Yet, the effects are larger for more extreme CRT values. Note that half of the observations fall outside the range mean ± one SD (see also Figure S1). Controlling for Raven does not alter these relationships (p = 0.01 and p = 0.02, respectively; see column [6] in Tables S4, S5), which again indicates an absence of mediation effects.

DISCUSSION

The dual-process approach of cognition has been recently suggested to reconcile previous conflictive findings on the relationship between creativity and executive cognition (Allen and Thomas, 2011; Ball et al., 2015; Barr et al., 2015; Sowden et al., 2015). We contribute to this literature by differentiating between the algorithmic and reflective minds (Evans and Stanovich, 2013), and by analyzing their separate effects on convergent thinking and four different dimensions of divergent thinking. We partially replicate the results of Barr et al. (2015) by finding that individuals' ability to make remote associations correlates positively with cognitive ability and cognitive reflection. However, we find that this effect on convergent thinking is mainly driven by cognitive ability. Similarly to Barr et al. (2015), we also find that higher levels of cognitive ability are related with higher originality scores and lower fluency scores in divergent thinking. Unlike Barr et al. (2015), we also analyze non-linear effects and find an inverted Ushape relationship between cognitive reflection and our measures of flexibility and fluency on the divergent thinking task. These new results suggest that individuals who are highly deliberative may have a disadvantage in producing a large number of new and creative ideas.

Dual-process models of creativity suggest that both generative and evaluative processes interact during the creative process (Finke et al., 1992; Basadur, 1995; Howard-Jones, 2002; Gabora, 2005; Nijstad et al., 2010; Gabora and Ranjan, 2013). Although these models do not have a straightforward mapping onto dualprocess models of cognition, the interaction between Type 1 and Type 2 cognitive processes may play a different role in different phases of the creative process. In this line, Sowden et al. (2015) call for future research "... *to investigate the extent to which creativity is deter-*

mined by the ability to shift between Type 1 and Type 2 thinking processes as a function of the circumstances and the stage of the creative processes" (p. 55). Our results suggest that cognitive reflection, that is the disposition to override automatic responses related to Type 1 processing and engage in Type 2 controlled thought, has a complex effect on divergent thinking. To some extent, cognitive reflection may be necessary to shift between the generative and evaluative processes involved in the production of new ideas. However, individuals characterized by high levels of reflection may be less able to rely on their intuitive, autonomous mind which can also be needed for unleashing one's creative power (e.g., Dorfman et al., 1996; Norris and Epstein, 2011; Jarosz et al., 2012).

The finding of an inverted U-shape relationship between cognitive reflection (and, analogously, intuitive processing) and creativity is consistent with recent advances on the "mad genius hypothesis": mild levels of top-down control dysfunction may be beneficial for creativity but severe impairment leads to poor creative performance (for a review, see Abraham, 2014).

Relatedly, neuropsychological research has shown an inverted-U shape relationship between spontaneous eye blink rates and *flexibility* in divergent creative thinking tasks (Chermahini and Hommel, 2010). To the extent that eye blink rates reflect dopaminergic activity (Karson, 1983), which is in turn linked to inhibitory control (Cohen and Servan-Schreiber, 1992), our results are in line with the finding of Chermahini and Hommel (2010).

Beyond its connection to basic cognitive research, our findings offer insights to managers in search for the creative talent of millennials. One essential implication of our study is that thinking too much may hamper important aspects of divergent creative thinking. This result is of primary relevance to hiring managers who may want to rely on cognitive reflection as the main criterion to recruit diligent (Corgnet et al., 2015b) and creative millennials. Our findings suggest that the cognitive tests used to recruit workers have to be adapted to the nature of the job offered. For example, recruiting for jobs that fundamentally require finding well-defined solutions to problems (such as accounting or actuarial jobs) can rely on a mix of cognitive ability and reflection tests which are good predictors of convergent creative thinking and diligence. However, recruiting for jobs that mainly require divergent creative thinking (such as marketing, industrial design, or psychology jobs) should not solely rely on cognitive measures. Recruiting based on cognitive reflection skills may actually prevent the hire of highly creative workers. These recommendations are becoming increasingly relevant as a growing number of jobs in modern economies require divergent creative thinking (Pink, 2005).

The current research has some necessary limitations that future research might remedy. To keep focus our study uses only one measure of fluid intelligence (Raven) and a single measure of cognitive style (CRT). Future research may assess the robustness of our findings to other measures of fluid intelligence and cognitive style, possibly extending the analysis to include crystallized intelligence. Also, our sample consisted entirely of undergraduates, with a limited age, education, and income range. Although this was a methodological choice that allowed us to study the workforce of the future, further studies may assess the robustness of our findings to different populations. Regarding our creativity measures, future research may attempt to extend our analysis to the case of practical creative tasks that are commonly encountered, for example, at the workplace. To that end, future research may embed the study of creativity in an organizational setting that allows for studying the relationship between workplace problem solving and cognitive skills.

On a methodological note, we used a fixed ordering of which may have influenced the results as, among other factors, fatigue may interfere with test results. While the 2-min break in the middle of the experiment might have mitigated spillover effects between the first and the second part of the experiment, concerns still remain. We encourage future research to explore possible ordering effects. In addition, future research focusing on state-level analyses of the role of intuition vs. reflection in creative performance is necessary to assess the robustness (and causality) of our trait-level findings as well as deepen our understanding of the cognitive basis of creativity. Along these lines, it would be interesting for future research to test the effect of cognitive manipulations such as cognitive load, ego depletion, priming, or time pressure/delay on creative performance. Our findings suggest that future research on the topic should attempt to capture potentially non-linear effects thus elaborating experimental designs that allow such effects to materialize. This can be done, for example, by considering at least three levels per treatment condition.

1. Do you agree that "too much" rational thought in some ways might preclude creativity?

2. Do you think that these research findings might apply only to millennials? Or, in your opinion, is this a multi-generational issue?

"REACHING THE MILLENNIAL GENERATION IN THE CLASSROOM," BY PAUL E. KOTZ, FROM THE *UNIVERSAL JOURNAL OF EDUCATIONAL RESEARCH*, 2016

ABSTRACT

The millennial generation (Generation Y) is the age group of children born between 1982 and 2002. Students aged 15 to 16 were asked to answer questions regarding their classroom experience. Sixty eight students were asked to participate in the survey and 63 gave consent for their participation. A qualitative survey approach was used asking three open ended questions, which yielded some fascinating findings, which complement the research that has been done on millennials. When a saturation point was reached, transcribing the same issue multiple times, the results were compiled and listed in narrative form. From this open-ended survey, and transcription of data, the results yielded that this group has a preference for order, safety and security, expect to talk more, and have engaging experiences while learning at the same time. Millennial students say they want to use the creative side of their brain. In the context of assisting teachers in the classrooms and future courses, instructors must realize that this millennial generation needs to be nurtured, mentored, developed, and released to grow in their own learning

KEYWORDS

Millennial, Qualitative, Creative, Mentoring, Engagement, Classroom, High School, Education, Teaching, Generation, Higher Education, College, University

1. INTRODUCTION

As an educator who has worked with high school for 15 years and universities for 23 years, I am continually trying to understand how to address the requests of the various current student sets. It is my desire to be aware and adjust my teaching style to make learning for these students richer and more accessible.

To this end, I asked 63 students within three independent sections of a private Midwest high school aged 15 to 16 to answer three survey questions regarding their classroom experience: *1. What could we as teachers do differently to make a student's experience better in the classroom? 2. What other tools do students need to be successful in the classroom?* And *3. Finally, what could I personally do better as a teacher?* I chose to focus on the first two questions for this article, reviewed and categorized the common ideas these students shared, and linked these themes with current research regarding millennials. I share these qualitative findings with the reader on teaching methods germane to the millennial student to shed additional light in management and marketing classrooms;

these young millennials will likely be the target group in our college and graduate schools.

2. BACKGROUND – REACHING THE MILLENNIAL GENERATION IN THE CLASSROOM

The millennial generation (also known as Generation Y) is the age group of children born between 1982 and 2002, some 81 million children who have taken over K-12, and have entered college and the workforce (Manning, [4] , p.1). This generation will replace the Baby-boomers as they retire.

Although this generation is not so very different from previous cohorts in the way they act and react to the world, they do have unique characteristics, some superficial, and some more deep-rooted. For example, millennials do not wear watches; because they all own cell phones that have this feature. Many do not read the newspaper, but prefer to acquire news on-line. Pictures taken by millennials are digitally stored and often placed on Facebook, or other social media. K-12 education, colleges and universities must adjust to the unique qualities of the millennial generation. This adjustment will aid millennials to become successful students in the classroom by educating in a way that is relevant and caters to their desire to engage in technology with educational tools and social media know-how.

As an educator who has worked with high school for 15 years and universities for 23 years, I am continually trying to understand how to address the requests of the various current student sets. It is my desire to be aware and adjust my teaching style to make learning for these students richer and more accessible.

3. LITERATURE REVIEW

Research indicates Millennials possess certain distinct characteristics.

The research indicates millennials desire having a closer relationship with parents. According to Elliott-Yeary [2], they admire their parents more than celebrities in 33% of the cases (p. 2). Millennials have grown up with a closer sphere of influence than ever before. Because they have grown up in a more dangerous world, society has created an environment where they are more sheltered, structured and live in a very protective atmosphere (Wilson and Gerber, [6], p.30).

These students want a close relationship with their teacher involving more guidance and extra personal attention. This group seems more respectful of others because they have grown up in a much more diverse world and a culture where "tolerance" is highly valued. Millennials have grown up in a society surrounded by different religions, races, ethnicities, and cultures. This may have contributed to more respect for these differences. In a crowded world where there are larger numbers of people in classrooms and activities, civility becomes even more essential to getting along and getting the most out of their education.

Some college administrators believe that many Gen Y's have "lost the sense of pure play." According to Allen [1], "They expect everything to be planned for them and do not expect to have as much freedom - or responsibility for structuring their educational lives" (p. 58). Wilson and Gerber [6] noticed that having spent a large percentage of time in structured activities, Millennials are accustomed to having a large amount of adult supervision. Thus, they may have poor self-management and conflict resolution skills (p.32).

Sometimes faculty finds the lack of authoritarian hierarchy in their study groups creates ambiguity concerning having a point of contact for information. At the same time, this group is open and eager to new experiences.

Students are responsive and "very smart" according to some faculty. Members of this cohort set the bar high for themselves, and they, like their Boomer parents, expect success. They sometimes "expect" to get good grades and are upset when this does not happen. As of 2002, "81% of college mental health service directors reported an increase in students with serious psychological problems" (Gallagher, [3]). Some counselors have identified these psychological problems as a result of the overwhelming pressure on students to succeed. The millennial group juggles many tasks at once. This generation often listens to music, works on the computer and watches television at the same time. This means they have come to expect stimulation in their learning environments and may be more focused than it seems to their teachers.

This group is socially conscious. There has been a resurgence of interest in politics and social issues among these young people. Lynch [4] reported, "70% of first-year students came to campus already registered to vote and 93% voted in the 2004 presidential election."

Millennials want to know what is expected and what criteria will be used to evaluate their performance. They are very likely to ask questions like, "Will this be on the test?" or "How is this going to affect my life in a positive way?"

Certainty and security is vital for this group. Tying learning outcomes to economic objectives is important for millennials.

Members of this group are motivated to learn ways of reducing stress and increasing their marketability. They place high value on developing good interpersonal skills and in getting along with their peers. It is a generation of readers, so written information works well with this group. Electronic books have in many cases replaced hard copies, and this group is adjusting to this new form of media.

4. METHODOLOGY

To this end, I asked 63 students within three independent sections of a private Midwest high school aged 15 to 16 to answer three survey questions regarding their classroom experience: See Appendix A. 1. What could we as teachers do differently to make a student's experience better in the classroom? 2. What other tools do students need to be successful in the classroom? And 3. Finally, what could I personally do better as a teacher? I chose to focus on the first two questions for this article, reviewed and categorized the common ideas these students shared, and linked these themes with current research regarding millennials. I share these qualitative findings with the reader on teaching methods germane to the millennial student to shed additional light in management and marketing classrooms; these young millennials will likely be the target group in our college and graduate schools.

A qualitative survey approach was used asking three open ended questions, which yielded some fascinating findings, which complement the research that has been done on millennials. When a saturation point was reached, transcribing the same issue more than seven times, the results were compiled and listed in narrative form below. A population of 68 students was survey, and 63 participated anonymously in this convenience sample. Three sections of students aged 15 to 16 were surveyed for a Midwestern high school.

5. RESULTS – WHAT THE SURVEY REVEALED IN THE DATA

Question 1: What Could We as Teachers Do Differently to Make Their Experience Better in the Classroom?

Young millennials aged 15-16, see the world in a completely different fashion than their Baby Boomer and Gen X predecessors. Millennials possess a wide array of talents and desire for creative outlets in the arts, hands-on activities, interactive games, video lectures, instructional demonstrations, field trips, colored worksheets and projects. Millennials also have a desire to learn in a more competitive fashion through games and interactive media.

Like most previous generations, millennials dislike homework but wish to be actively engaged in class and use their time wisely. Wilson and Gerber (2008) recognize millennials prefer to work in small groups with music playing in the background instead of working alone in a silent classroom. Stimulation is a motivator for many in this generation (p.34).

This group has a preference for order, safety and security. They expect to talk more and have engaging experiences that allow them to learn at the same time. Staying interested is vitally important to this group. As always, there are individual members of this generation who like to work independently and do not like to present in class. In surveys given to these young students, time and time again they emphasize making things fun and more "interesting." At the same time, they see the need for maintaining a quiet time to hear instructions and brief lectures to initiate the tasks for the day. Silence and the ability to have clear, complete notes is still a prerequisite for success. They have no problem with being active thinkers within their preferred environment. They express a need to see honesty and understand why things are the way they are.

Millennials are a group that values individual attention and ideas that are fully explained. Students ask for shorter assignments that include more depth and prefer homework assignments that are spaced out with flexible time. They strongly favor activities over lectures. Repetition to enable mastery is a desire for this group. If an activity does not particularly suit their interest, a teacher or facilitator may lose students' focus. Students ask for teachers to facilitate their note taking so that they can remain organized. This group expects mentors and adults to have patience with them and remain flexible.

Millennial students critique their own peers saying their generation is not very focused. Some have asked instructors to close the doors to experience fewer distractions from people in hallways. They acknowledge that each of us has different learning styles, but smaller groups are more attractive to them than large groups or working individually. Some students suggest they need to be more positive, determined, motivated, disciplined and possess more self-control; they do not want to cause distractions for the facilitator/teacher.

Question 2: What Other Tools Do They Need to Be Successful in the Classroom?

Millennial students say they want to use both sides of their brain, especially their creative side. Some say they want to do what is enjoyable in their own estimation. They asked for more comfortable chairs because they sit in classrooms, in many cases, for six to seven periods per day. Comfortable, welcoming and flexible spaces are very important to this group.

Since they employ laptops, they wish for schools to find additional, better ways to learn online. When videos and movies have relevance to the course, students appreciate the opportunity to do this media learning at home followed by the opportunity to ask questions in the next class (flipped curriculum). Students recognize their own visual learning skill and wish instructors would recognize this and teach to this style. Students repeatedly request more interactive materials, additional visuals and more personal involvement.

Students also want to ensure fairness, want to matter in the group, and be acknowledged for their strengths. A cluster of this generation enjoys interactive games, quizlets, and other approaches that help review concepts in alternative forms to lecture. They ask for open notes on examinations, and more hands-on activities. They wish for adults to have patience with their active "multilayered brains," and that teachers would be sympathetic to their need to know why and how projects are to be done. They do not like to rush through lessons. This includes longer review sessions and the desire for thoroughness.

Some students say that teachers or facilitators should do a better job of staying on topic. While in the minority, some students have said that computers should not be allowed in the classroom. While they are similar to students of previous generations, they have used technology since they were infants, and are "wired" as no other previous group of students. This presents particular challenges and opportunities in teaching to millennials.

6. CONCLUSIONS – HOW DO WE TEACH TO THIS GROUP?

Keeping this group interested by introducing a topic that taps into a personal interest is a primary way of reaching millennials in an educational format. Students repeatedly comment that relating lessons to topics of interest makes their learning experience that much better. This can be problematic because it is difficult for one or two instructors in a classroom to meet the personal interests for each individual. Lynch [4] emphasizes "there is a growing mismatch between faculty and students in terms of teaching and learning."

Small group discussions, projects, in-class presentations and debates, peer critiques, team projects, service learning, field experiences, developing simulations, and case method approaches have been found to be successful for high school and college millennial students. Millennial students seem to thrive when they excel collaboratively while still keeping their unique personal approaches intact.

The development of "learning communities," (small groups of students who can discuss and analyze readings and assignments) is beneficial and should be encouraged. These learning communities also address the need of many millennial students for hands-on activity in the classroom. Having grown up in a highly structured world, this group prefers cohesiveness to ambiguity. Millennials look for such structure in their learning settings. They want to know precisely what is required, when work is due, and very specific information about expectations.

Providing frequent feedback is essential for Generation Y to move to the next step and progress as learners. This feedback allows them to know when they are headed in the right direction and when they are getting off-track. Frequent attention from teachers is welcome. According to Elliot-Yeary [2], "Millennials want to enjoy their learning. If it is not fun, it will be cast into the category of boring and may become less effective." Millennials learn best when they are entertained.

This group wants to fully employ their talents. This is a generation that likes to be useful and helpful. When students know more about a topic an instructor might allow them discuss it in depth.

7. RECOMMENDATIONS

Tying learning tasks to real-world problems is essential to these learners. If a subject is not seen as relevant, there may be resistance to learning. The need for connections between applications in the world and practice continues to be a theme of which this generation approves. These students also value convenience and want supplies to be readily available in the classroom. Additional recommendations might include answering some of the following questions: How are these unique to this generation versus others? After an examination of both survey questions and the research, the question must still be addressed: What makes these people tick? Are people's learning needs truly the same no matter what generation they come from? The millennial generation may need more discipline and the realization that satisfaction does not come quickly, but with hard work. In the context of business management and marketing courses, the adults of the earlier generations may remember what it was like to arrive at young adulthood. They must also realize that this millennial generation needs to be nurtured, mentored, developed, and released to grow in their own learning. According to Elliot-Yeary [2] "This generation is as comfortable with technology as a fish is with water." The hybrid models cropping up at many colleges and universities offer flexibility to learn in the brick and mortar environment on one weekend, and work on-line the next. This may give the working professional a chance to use both technology and interpersonal skills with other colleagues in face-to-face dialogue and collaboration. At the same time, this technology does not necessarily change the student, just the perspective of the learning.

Millennials' reliance on Facebook for political news has clear implications for political candidates – and for campaign spending. As I've noted before, experts estimate that only about 3% of campaign ad dollars are spent on digital – maybe more in presidential elections. In the future, this is obviously bound to grow – but how rapidly and by how much and? Millennials still punch below their weight in terms of voter turnout, but as they age (and, presumably, vote more) this trend towards social media will have an impact.

We should expect to see even more micro-targeting. During the 2012 elections, the New York Times noted how "in recent primaries, two kinds of Republican voters have been seeing two different Mitt Romney video ads pop up on local and national news Web sites." A former campaign manager for President Obama recently noted of his experience with U.K. elections – where social media are already dominant given much tighter regulations on campaign finance and ad buys – that "Facebook and other social media, was the most effective because it was often a message shared by their friends or others they trusted versus politicians and the media that they don't trust. We found that the undecided voters were moving our way as a result."

What does the trend toward social media mean for the finances of already beleaguered media platforms? And for campaign regulation? Local TV has been one of the few journalism platforms to see increasing ad revenues in recent years, while newspaper and magazine revenues have cratered. This is in large part because of political advertising, which tends to happen on news-producing local TV stations. What will happen to the sustainability of local TV news as campaign advertising and communication are increasingly transferred to social media intermediaries rather than news content producers? And, with television traditionally positioned as the primary channel for campaign communications, current campaign finance laws and regulations are heavily oriented around broadcasting. The FEC has struggled with how to regulate this shift toward digital campaigning.

Millennials may be living in less of an echo chamber – for now. The jury is still out on what role social media plays in determining who sees what news (even if unconsciously). In the Pew Research survey, only 18% of Millennials who pay attention to political posts say the posts they see on Facebook are "mostly or always in line with their own views" (versus 21% of Gen Xers and 31% of Baby Boomers). Twitter and Facebook algorithms remain proprietary. Recent and hotly contested research by Facebook's data scientists finds that the biggest determinant of what news you see is who your friends are, rather than a social media algorithm, and for most people only about 20% of "friends" are from an opposing party. Earlier 2010 research (below) makes similar suggestions regarding the role of the internet, versus other media and interactions (e.g., with personal acquaintances), in influencing "ideological segregation." That said, if the aforementioned Facebook study is right, algorithms may cause as much as a 4% to 10% *decrease* in ideologically "cross-cutting" exposure on that site. While not a huge amount, that means Facebook – if willing – could make itself part of the solution to echo chambers, rather than part of the problem.

What does the rise of social media mean in the long term for an informed and engaged citizenry? The folks at

Pew Research Center note how hard it is to understand: "The [social media] experience is individualized through one's own choices, through the friends in one's network and their proclivities, and through algorithms – all of which can change over time." As they report, we are just starting to understand these interactions, and the implications they will have for American politics.

1. Do you think that Facebook or Twitter is better for following political news? Why?

2. Is there a drawback to relying on social media for news? What might it be?

"HOW SEXTING IS CREATING A SAFE SPACE FOR CURIOUS MILLENNIALS," BY MELISSA MEYER, FROM *THE CONVERSATION* WITH THE UNIVERSITY OF CAPE TOWN, MARCH 21, 2016

Millennials have become cyborgs. They exist far beyond biology and through a variety of technological devices which don't function as external entities but as a platform and backdrop to their daily lives. They were born between 1980 and 2000, and are regarded by researchers as an open-minded, responsive and liberal generation who believe that "useful is the new cool". They've grown up in an "always-on" digital era: the online world is their platform for communication and expression

So it should be no wonder that, in addition to social and professional online existence, they also express their sexuality via technology. Social media applications like WhatsApp have created a new avenue for curious young people to explore, express and develop their sexuality. Sexting – exchanging texts, photos and videos of a sexual nature – has become so commonplace that many millennials consider it a normal and even healthy part of a relationship.

But some people are horrified by the idea of sexting. Are they right to panic?

The short answer is no. Firstly, sexting is often a safer alternative to physical sex, without the risks of STIs and pregnancy. And, importantly, my research has revealed that it is primarily a feminist space: when used correctly it offers both partners equal power to start, stop and direct the interaction. Young women felt comfortable with sexting because it diminished their risk of being over-powered or pressured into non-consensual sex.

MILLENNIALS' OWN EXPERIENCES

A recent study has started steering sexting research in a new direction that has millennials' experiences and opinions as its base. This is important, as much of the literature currently circulating does not employ appropriate research methods or is biased towards finding the harm in this new moral panic that's "corrupting our youth".

My own research, too, has focused on millennials' attitudes to and practice of sexting. I collected the data from 579 students aged between 18 and 30 in an online survey at the University of Cape Town in South Africa. I also conducted a number of focus groups. Here's what I found:

- Millennials consider sexting fun and flirty.
- They use it to get positive feedback and boost their self-esteem.
- 55% of the respondents said they had friends who sext with nude or semi-nude pictures; 53% have done so themselves and 59% have received such content.
- It is not necessarily a private activity – 57% of male and 44% of female student respondents have seen someone else's private naked or semi-naked picture(s). So much so, that 72% expressed the fear of someone else seeing their picture as a serious concern or hindrance to sexting.
- Importantly, millennials were highly aware of the risks posed by sexting. They also understood how it could be potentially harmful, but most said that the benefits outweighed the risks.
- Participants said that the most common risk associated with sexting, apart from leaked photos, is receiving an unsolicited and unexpected sext, especially one of a graphic, sexual nature. This is an especially common complaint among young women, and leaves the receiver feeling violated, but also with the expectation to respond.
- Some were also concerned about the turn-taking repertoire of sexting, which means that when one receives a sext it creates the expectation of returning a similar contribution. If you receive a photo of your partner's naked torso, for instance, a text or photo of your face is not considered an appropriate

response. For inexperienced sexters, this could create negative pressure.

SEXTING TO BUILD INTIMACY

Part of my research focused on *why* millennials sext. I found that it is most prevalent among couples, people in long-distance relationships and, interestingly, virgin teens. These experiences were discussed in the focus groups, where students could elaborate on the answers they'd given in the survey.

Sexting is likely to happen before sex, as a way to get to know one's partner sexually and to build intimacy. This explains why high school pupils who still identify as virgins would sext: to them, it's a way to bridge the gap of distance between two interested, consenting partners who wish to be intimate, experiment or are just curious and wish to explore their sexuality. All of this can happen in the safety and comfort of their own rooms with the power to stop the interaction at any time.

It is exactly this power which, from a cyberfeminist theoretical point of view, makes sexting so appealing – especially to young women. Sexting is a turn-taking, co-authoring process. Both parties contribute equally and have equal stakes in the outcome. Both partners have the power to sway the story and to back out if they feel uncomfortable. It is a space that allows both parties to ask for what they want, explain what they dislike and get the satisfaction they desire by giving the other what they want.

Sexting has the potential to be liberating and empowering if used correctly. It can bring two partners together through an intimacy otherwise denied by distance. But sexters – and particularly young millennials – need to be taught how to navigate these sometimes murky waters.

BREAKING TABOOS

Schools and the popular media need to start addressing issues around consent and non-consensual sharing. These sorts of interventions will teach young people to use potential sexting platforms appropriately. They'll learn how to deal better with situations of unwanted pressure, abuse (such as receiving an unsolicited nude picture) and more broadly about their rights, how to protect themselves and when to ask for help.

Millennials also need to learn how technology can be used in an empowering way. This may be tougher in poorer countries or regions where economic access and exposure to technology is racialised, genderised and stratified by ethnicity. An inexperienced user, or one who doesn't fit the typical Western, empowered millennial prototype – or match people's ideas of a savvy, connected "digital native" – might fall back on traditional constraints. These constraints paint men as more dominating and women as submissive and unwilling to displease their lovers.

Such programmes and learning can only happen once the taboo of sexting is lifted. This will require a dialogue between millennials, parents and educators, and a space for millennials' own views on the subject to be heard.

1. What do you think about the first sentence of this article: "Millennials have become cyborgs"? What does the author mean by this? Do you agree or disagree?

2. Why does the author consider that sexting might create a "feminist space" for safe sexual experimentation? Do you agree or disagree?

CHAPTER 6

HOW WILL MILLENNIALS SHAPE THE FUTURE?

With the oldest millennials firmly in adulthood and the youngest soon entering the workforce, this generation is on the verge of becoming leaders in the United States and around the world. As millennials establish themselves in fields like the media, politics, medicine, and law, their values and views will shape the future. But for a generation that has struggled economically and has shown a willingness to break with tradition, what might that future look like? In this chapter, we'll look at some of the ways millennials are already making their mark, what the past can tell us about the impact a young and engaged population can have on the future of their country, and how this generation is going to change the world.

"REPORT SHOWS WHOOPING $8.8 TRILLION CLIMATE TAB BEING LEFT FOR NEXT GENERATION," BY LAUREN MCCAULEY, FROM *COMMON DREAMS*, AUGUST 22, 2016

"We do not inherit the Earth from our ancestors, we borrow it from our children," is an oft-quoted proverb, frequently used to explain the importance of environmental preservation. Unsaid, however, is how much it will impact the next generation if the Earth is bequeathed in a lesser state.

Environmental campaigners NextGen Climate and public policy group Demos published a new study that attempts to quantify the true cost of not addressing climate change to the millennial generation and their children.

The Price Tag of Being Young: Climate Change and Millennials' Economic Future compares some of the high costs millennials will face in the "new inequality economy"—such as student debt, child care costs, stagnant wages, as well as financial and job insecurity—against the fiscal impacts of unmitigated global warming.

"The fact is," the report states, "unchecked climate change will impose heavy costs on millennials and subsequent generations, both directly in the form of reduced incomes and wealth, and indirectly through likely higher tax bills as extreme weather, rising sea levels, drought, heat-related health problems, and many other climate change-related problems take their toll on our society."

The impacts from climate costs alone, the report finds, are "comparable to Great Depression-era losses." The study employs a model developed by researchers from Stanford University and University of California at Berkeley that measures the effects of rising temperatures on long-term economic growth and national productivity drawing on 50 years of data from 166 countries.

The "no climate action" scenario found that by 2100 global per capita GDP will shrink by 23 percent relative to a scenario without climate change. The U.S. is estimated to take a 5 percent hit by 2050 that jumps to 36 percent by 2100 should no climate action occur.

This adds up to a loss of nearly $8.8 trillion in lifetime income for millennials and tens of trillions for their children.

In comparison, the cost of climate inaction over-shadows the significant losses from other economic burdens, such as student debt. The report states:

> According to Demos calculations, for a median-earning college graduate with median student debt, the lifetime wealth loss due to student debt is approximately $113,000, which is 40 percent less than the $187,000 lifetime wealth loss of a college-educated, median-earning 21-year-old if we fail to act on climate change.

But when these myriad forces are stacked together, they add up to a staggering burden. The report further highlights how climate inaction only exacerbates preexisting inequality:

> Communities of color and low-income communities will be hit the hardest, as these communities have fewer resources to deal with the impacts of climate

change [...]. Further, these same communities have always had the highest exposure to coal-burning power plants and other sources of fossil fuel pollution, with sharply negative health impacts [...]

If the transition to a clean energy economy is delayed, or if it is implemented unequally in keeping with historical patterns of racial exclusion, the fossil fuel economy will only deepen its toll on the health and well-being of America's poorest and most vulnerable communities.

What's more, the report notes, "the economic risks are compounded even further since inaction on climate change means that we are missing out on a major opportunity for much-needed new investment and millions of new jobs by transitioning to clean energy."

"For the millennial generation," the study concludes, "today's status quo on climate and inequality is not only unjust but it is also unsustainable."

Democratic heavyweight and NextGen Climate president Tom Steyer said the report underscores the importance of the upcoming presidential election between Democratic nominee Hillary Clinton and Republican Donald Trump.

"When we look at the consequences of this election, the choice between the candidates could not be more stark," Steyer said, "and the voice of millennial voters has never been more important."

Sara Jordan, policy manager at NextGen Climate agreed, writing, "Millennials have the numbers to elect climate champions this fall, but we have to show up to vote. Our future depends on it."

1. What big issues do you think millennials should be particularly concerned about? Why?

2. Do you think that issues that may affect one generation more than another can stand as a rallying point for that generation? Why or why not?

"HOW TO LEISURE LIKE A LAZY MILLENNIAL," BY EILEEN L. WITTIG, FROM THE FOUNDATION FOR ECONOMIC FREEDOM, JANUARY 5, 2017

You've done it. You've made it through the work week, through the traffic, and you've made it home. You unlock your door and wonder again how long it will take until these stupid keys are replaced with what cars already have – the ability to unlock when you get within a certain radius of the door, and the ability to open when you kick the bottom of the door. I mean really, how do they expect you to juggle your keys *and* the nachos stuff you got in preparation for the weekend?

You enter your home and your phone automatically pairs to your speaker, because ain't nobody got time for those stupid auxiliary cords. It starts playing "Closer" by the Chainsmokers because you were listening to it on repeat on the way home, but you're ready for something else now. "Alexa," you say, "play something else."

"Okay," your speaker says, and "Starboy" by The Weeknd comes on. Perfect. "Alexa, turn on the lights." Let there be light, indeed.

You dump your cross-body work bag on your clean floor, vacuumed by your Roomba. It just found its way into your bedroom, shark fin attached because you were bored that one time. Alright yes it was inspired by that YouTube video of the cat in a shark costume riding a Roomba around the room.

Immediately, you change into the comfiest clothes you own, which could mean sweatpants and a t-shirt from high school, or legit pajamas. Jeans are not on this list, and neither is anything else you're willing to be caught dead in.

BON APPETIT

One hour later, your significant other makes it through the traffic and to your door. By this time you've settled into your pre-Netflix routine of checking three social media platforms simultaneously while not really listening to the music that's still playing, and your SO plops onto your couch next to you to join in (on their own phone of course). You trade stories about former roommates and teammates for a while before realizing that you don't have drinks.

You get up to fix this terrible problem when you find out you have a worse one – you are out of alcohol, and you only have flat soda for a mixer. And you're in your comfy clothes, and there's no going out once you've entered that stage. After a moment of panic you remember what year it is, and you take out your phone to order alcohol to be delivered. Crisis averted.

But this makes you think that by the time the alcohol gets there, you're going to be hungry, so you go back and forth about what you don't want for dinner until you settle on Curry (you're sick of pizza because you've been eating leftover pizza for lunch at work for about three days).

"Alexa, ask what beer goes with Curry." "Here's what I found for furry deer," she responds. "Cancel," you sigh, and order whatever beer you feel like. You turn on *Bob's Burgers* to watch while you wait because watching a show which takes place in a restaurant half the time is a really great idea when you're hungry.

A couple episodes later, just as you're starting to get hangry, your food and drinks arrive. The two of you sit down on your couch to eat. You don't have a dining room/kitchen/breakfast table, because where would you put it? Besides, why would you eat at a table when you have a couch that's much comfier and conveniently angled towards your smart TV?

After complaining about That Guy At The Office and That One Chick, respectively, you and your significant other start the same discussion you had for dinner – what you don't want to watch on Netflix. Ten minutes and dozens of exasperated eyerolls later, you end up rewatching *Peaky Blinders* because you're cultured like that, you have to wait another month before the slew of new show seasons starts, and you still have to wait two more days for the next episode of *Sherlock*. As you start the show, your smart lightbulbs sync to your TV and your apartment is bathed in color-coordinated lighting, depending on the scene of the show (lots of gray and brown, since it's *Peaky Blinders*).

Once in a while you interrupt the show to point out something in an article you've been reading even as you're watching Netflix, because heaven forbid you do one thing at a time. Or you show them a recipe you found on Pinterest, which sounds delicious even though you just ate. It makes you hungry, again, and you decide to make brownies from the mix that was delivered to you yesterday via Amazon Prime Now. You long for the day your brownie mix will be delivered in one hour instead of two and dropped onto your balcony via drone instead of at your door by an actual person, because Ugh People.

SWEET SLUMBER

Several episodes, drinks, and brownies later, you fall asleep on your significant other's shoulder. They shake you awake and suggest you both give in and go to bed, and you get very excited at the thought of finally being able to sleep without having to go to work again in the morning (five nights is a long wait for this). But first, you head to the bathroom and brush your teeth with your electric toothbrush that tells you when you've brushed an area long enough and yells at you when you're pressing too hard on your gums.

Finally, your lights turn themselves off as you shut your door, you fall onto your mattress that arrived in a vacuum-sealed bag in a box, tell your phone to cancel your alarm for the morning, set your sleeping app to wake you at your lightest moment of sleep sometime between 8 a.m. and 11 a.m., and are dead to the world.

1. Do you think this is a fair and accurate representation of many millennials' lives? Why or why not?

2. How might a millennial's economic status or social class play into the imagined scenario here?

"OUTSIDE RNC HEADQUARTERS, MILLENNIALS DECLARE: 'IT'S TRUMP VS. ALL OF US'," BY DEIRDRE FULTON, FROM *COMMON DREAMS*, OCTOBER 6, 2016

A group of multiracial millennials gathered outside the Republican National Committee's (RNC) headquarters on Thursday afternoon, demanding party chair Reince Priebus withdraw his support for GOP presidential nominee Donald Trump and reject what they call "a 50-year strategy of using racism for electoral gain."

Under the banner #AllOfUs2016, the young people are seeking to show Republicans and the media alike: "America is for all of us. Our generation will fight for an America with liberty, freedom, and justice for all."

"I'm sick and tired of the Republican Party, a party of racists and billionaires, running our country into the ground," Anthony Torres, a 22-year-old Latino organizer living in Washington, D.C., told *Common Dreams* ahead of Thursday's action.

"A Donald Trump presidency," he said, "would normalize overt white supremacy, put my family and my communities in greater danger, and really threaten much of what you see our generation fighting for"—including climate justice, the movement for black lives, the struggle to end deportations, and what Torres described as "a real political revolution."

Just this week, added 25-year-old Waleed Shahid in an interview, vice-presidential nominee Mike Pence demonstrated how supposedly "mainstream" Republicans plan to address Trump's controversial campaign: "Look away, pretend it doesn't exist, and make excuses for it."

"What Mike Pence did at the debate," Shahid said, was show that "Republican leaders [are] getting in line to back his hatred."

Thursday's press conference comes on the heels of a sit-in at House Speaker Paul Ryan's office last month, which saw several arrests as the same contingent called for Ryan to reject Trump and the GOP's "dog-whistle racism."

That message apparently fell on deaf ears, as Ryan's re-election campaign announced Thursday that he'll appear with Trump this weekend in Wisconsin. In a piece titled, "Paul Ryan Burns Final Shred Of Dignity, Will Campaign With Trump," the *Huffington Post* reported that "It's the first time the two will appear together since the Republican National Convention in July."

Shahid, who took part in the September sit-in, said Ryan's actions show he is "choosing votes and his party over the future of our democracy."

Both Ryan and Priebus, Shahid said, "actually know that Donald Trump is a huge threat to America, and a huge threat to American democracy, but they're too afraid and too selfish to do anything about it."

"Paul Ryan and the Republican Party always talk about how much they love America and how patriotic they are," he said, "but if they really loved America that much, I think they would stand to defend our democracy against Trump's hateful and fascist campaign."

1. This article was written before Donald Trump was elected President of the United States in 2016. How do you feel millennials' political role has changed since the election?

2. Millennials tend to be more politically liberal than other generations. Do you think this is a function of age or issues?

"HOW TO FIX WORK/LIFE BALANCE FOR CONSTANTLY CONNECTED MILLENNIALS," BY PAUL LEVY, FROM *THE CONVERSATION*, JULY 15, 2015

There's a paradox sitting at the heart of the issue of work/life balance at the moment.

Research shows that people are increasingly seeking 24-7 digital connection while driving; in the bedroom; and in social and family lives.

More and more people sleep next to their phones, take devices on dates and digitally connect at meal times. Many people want to be "always on". But when you're open and available, it's hard to choose to ignore it when the emails happen to be from the office or the tweets are coming from the boss.

OLD RULES

The concept of work/life balance largely precedes the advent of digital technology. The term was first coined in the 1970s, but 100 years ago, employees were taking papers home their work finished up.

Round-the-clock digital response and connection is much more pervasive. Research suggests that many millennials want their home life to be just that, in fact, 100% that. One global study of full-time workers in eight countries conducted by Ernst & Young finds that millennials – and particularly millennial parents – are so serious about finding work/life balance, they're willing to relocate if it means they can move into a job that offers it.

This is only one snapshot, but there's a lot of research around at the moment about work/life balance. Employees want to bring their own devices to work, and enjoy social media connection in whatever way suits them. But they want to close the door on work when they get home and not be pestered by work at home. And they are serious about it. The Ernst & Young study found:

> *Millennials in the survey are also more willing than other generations to pass up a promotion, change jobs, take a pay cut, or even change careers in order to achieve more flexibility.*

So, here's the paradox: People are encouraged to bring their own devices to work and yet many of those people who want to check personal updates at work don't want it to work in the other direction. But it is hard to resist: the technology is an enabler of a poor work/life balance, and precedents are quickly established.

DIGITAL NATIVES

The digitally native generation are more than able and used to taking devices home with them. A survey by Workfront found that 22% of baby boomers in the 55-64 age bracket thought it was OK to answer a work email during dinner. Ask 18-34-year-old millennials though, and that shoots up to 52%. More than half of adults questioned in a 60 Minutes/Vanity Fair survey, meanwhile, said monitoring emails outside office hours was routine.

And so it seems that millennials who have become used to this constant digital connection are increasingly pushing back, even to the point of stepping away from the organisations who force it upon them. Evidence for dissatisfaction is growing.

Almost two-thirds of fathers who have youngsters under school age do not have a work pattern that suits them, according to a Guardian survey. Half the respondents were worried that requests for flexible or home working would be seen as a "lack of commitment".

LEFT TO THEIR OWN DEVICES

This offers a challenge to employers, particularly as it makes offering staff a work/life balance – in an age when it has never been harder – a key weapon in staff retention and attraction, at least, according to the Randstad Award employer branding research study. Finding and retaining the best millennial talent requires a genuine adaptability and sensitivity to the issue, and an ability to navigate a way past the "always-on" ubiquity of technology.

So, how are leaders and business owners attempting to resolve this paradox? My own research suggests that an increasing number of businesses are no longer managing staff by clocking their working hours but instead by co-ordinating by what organisational Canadian writer Henry Mintzberg calls "standardised outputs and values". We agree goals and core values with employees from the outset and then leave it to them to complete their work in whatever ways suit them.

This is a very "millennial" way of working. It isn't that millennials don't want to take work home. It is more that they want to decide their own work/life balance. They don't want taking work home to be the default position. According to a new survey of nearly 10,000 workers in eight countries by Ernst & Young's Global Generations Research: "Younger workers see that technology frees them to work productively from anywhere."

Maybe it is the attempt to incorporate this modern approach into traditional working patterns that causes the problems? It might just be a case of all or nothing to make it work.

BOUNDARY REVIEW

We can the paradox by putting the control of working flexibly into the hands of workers after agreeing the underlying values and goals. Work/life balance then becomes about freely working in different physical places, whilst mobile, on different devices and via flexible platforms. Just because we can bring our own devices to work, doesn't mean we have to bring our work home.

In practice that means higher degrees of trust. It isn't about micro-managing staff time and physical place, but current research suggests that is still largely going on. To succeed here, and for companies to get the right levels of performance out of their staff, it becomes about plug and play work processes, about porting content across platforms and devices, about respecting the boundaries between home and work and designing business processes that embed that respect. It means going the whole hog. Total flexibility to get the best out of agile technologies and trust to empower your flexible workers.

1. With flexibility often comes fewer boundaries between work and home. Do you think this is a necessary tradeoff?

2. Do you think that millennials will change the way they and future generations work? In what way?

"MILLENNIALS ARE ON THE MARCH," BY SAM RETROSI, FROM *SOCIALIST WORKER*, MARCH 11, 2014

The mass arrest of 398 Keystone XL activists outside the White House on March 2 consisted primarily of youth--college students and members of other organizations heavily populated by the millennial generation.

Thousands of young people gathered under the banner of #XL Dissent to demand the Obama administration finally reject the Keystone XL tar sands pipeline. Hundreds among the group committed to directly challenge the state in an act of mass civil disobedience. Mounting the White House fence, we secured ourselves with zip ties, many of us hand-in-hand. As police surrounded the area, barricading us in, we stood warmed by the spirit of collective dissent, blissful in an experience of community that the larger system has all too often deprived us of.

Though initial weather conditions were relatively mild, as an impending winter storm system began to set in, temperatures began to drop. Cold rain started to fall with increasing strength. Nearby, police stood guard in rain gear, steaming cups of coffee in hand. Immobilized by the zip ties that secured us to the fence, though we were able to maintain our resolve, we weren't able to prevent body temperatures from falling.

A rumbling arose from the crowd, hanging ominously over the detainment area. Most were well aware that weather conditions had been slated to worsen--what we weren't prepared for was a war of attrition waged by institutionalized authority who had decided we needed a collective slap on the wrist.

After several hours, the mass arrests began. Reflective of the individualization we have been subjected to in society at large, the hundreds assembled were forced through processing one-by-one, undergoing a systematic separation from the collective.

Biff Anderson, a member of the ecosocialist contingent organized by the System Change Not Climate Change coalition reflected back on previous experience with mass arrest:

This is intentional. We are being disciplined. Mass arrests are not usually this slow. These people, are dressed for the 50 or 60 degree weather that was forecast. Now they are visibly shivering and turning blue at the lips. This is an anecdotal reminder that the barbarism of a system that starves 90 million children to death globally each year on a planet that is home to 7 billion people, yet produces enough food to feed 10 billion people, is not human nature.

It is because of the profit motive. Massive profit for a few at the expense of everyone else. If given accurate information and a real say in how the world is organized for human need, humanity would vote a resounding NO on things like the Keystone XL pipeline with no second-guessing.

As some police stood in warm tents, slowly filtering activists into nearby vehicles that waited to transport us to a jail in Anacostia, others began to filter into the throng of rumbling activists, admonishing the wayward youth. One shivering young woman, teeth chattering, face blue, all 110 pounds, with her hair, body and clothing soaked, gritted her teeth, looking up defiantly into the face of an officer who said, "Maybe you should have checked the weather, maybe you should have reconsidered this action, maybe you're learning your lesson. "

Others, detained for upwards of four hours, began to feel the pull of other inevitable physical needs. One man begged to use the bathroom, even assured the officer to whom he appealed that he would return, that one of the officials standing idly by could accompany him the nearest restroom. The automatic response was, "That's too bad, you're just going to have to go in your pants."

Miserable, cold, facing an unknown period of time stretching ahead before they could be processed, activists lined up along the fence began to put their heads together to figure out how best to manage the conditions. The consensus among most was that warmth could not be maintained in such a stationary position, that the best thing to do would be to liberate ourselves from the zip ties that bound us to the White House fence inside our enclosure.

Once off the fence, some began to dance, skip, or do jumping jacks in order to warm their soaked bodies. Most began to migrate toward one another, forming collective sources of warmth, shifting those shivering most violently toward the center of the huddle. Some who could spare an extra layer shed them, passing additional clothing on to still the chattering teeth of those who weren't faring so well. As the cold subsided, despite the fact that we had been warmed by one another, body heat restored, we stayed packed together, enjoying the feeling of closeness to others that our society so often deprives us of.

Tied to the fence, freezing collectively in individual isolation, we proved that we couldn't be diverted from the task at hand. We were not seduced by temporary comforts that would disband our collective resolve, beckoning from the world outside of our Sunday trial. The seductive allure of a warm spot of respite for one loomed shallow and meaningless if it couldn't be had by all. So we found the solution in the moment in coming together, rather than piecing off in search of the warmth we might find by embracing individual self-interest.

We pushed past the false promise of the comforts we've been told we could have. We saw the possibility of individual comfort for one in its true form: the death of protection delivered by the collective. We know intuitively that the collective is something we ourselves give life to, and is thus more secure than asking for protection and resources to be delivered from above. It is this clarity with which we are coming to see the political promises of the elite as lies: meaningless platitudes designed to stifle any voice calling for the real social--"change" we were promised one too many times.

The millennial generation has been forced into an atomized society rife with externally imposed, class-based state and economic control. Though forced to integrate into such a society, this is not our creation. Still, we have been told to deal with the crises it has generated.

The Keystone XL Pipeline is just one of these crises, holding the promise of environmental devastation that will visit our future in innumerable ways. When left to their own devices today's youth are showing up to provide a few lessons for those who have decided we have much to learn and accept from their deficient example.

In those few situations within which we are enabled even momentarily to exercise agency, most of which can only be found in the act of dissent, humans communally and cooperatively make decisions that benefit the majority. It is clear that if millennials desire a better future than the legacy of dysfunction and inequality handed down from above, they will have to join with others, resorting to collective devices.

Such action will not be defined by the mandates of "empowerment" by way of "personal responsibility" and "self-actualization." Like the majority of society, today's youth can and must look to dissent, to the power found in one another, something that this weekend proves they are all too capable of doing.

The scarring intellectual impact of corporate education reform cannot be understated. The millennial generation is the direct recipient of this form of public policy. As the first downwardly mobile generation in U.S. history, these citizens are the recipients of post-recession economic hardships that play out in places like the job market, the university, our health care system, even in the precarious nature of the damaged environment of the world they have been given to inhabit.

But this generational inequality also takes on ideological and psychological dimensions that are a product of a market-centric, technologically oriented advanced stage of neoliberal capitalism. As a result of forced integration into a system that mandates standardization of thought, uniformity of action, obedience, self-reliance, and the intake of mass amounts of shallow information, millennials have been forced to absorb mental constructs that are designed to impede cooperative forms of critical thought.

Yet if XL Dissent proves anything, it's that we retain the inner will to see the truth behind supposedly legitimate authority and to reject it. If we desire for a better world, a better future for ourselves and generations to come, we cannot hope to inherit such an order. We must fight for it.

Contrary to the image sold in the mass media of what characterizes the youth of today, many know on which side their bread is buttered. The interests of the majority do not lie in obedient integration into the system that is destroying our environment along with all other hopes for a bright future. We have been disappointed one too many times. We are falling into a spiral of downward mobility within which we can never hope for the kind of stability we experienced during the economic era of our upbringing. We are drowning in a pool of student debt and we face a highly uncertain job market.

In light of all this, we are starting to see where real hope can be realized. The theater in which actual social change can be pursued is nothing short of collective action and solidarity. If we will be deprived of community we will form our own communities of resistance. An end to climate change will only be found in system change. And system change will be found in one another.

1. The author refers to millennials as the first "downwardly mobile generation in US history." Do you agree with the author that this will change millennials' political views?

2. Why did so many millennials, in particular, oppose the Keystone XL pipeline?

"KRISTEN SOLTIS ANDERSON: CAN REPUBLICANS WIN MILLENNIALS IN 2016?" BY NILAGIA MCCOY, FROM THE SHORENSTEIN CENTER ON MEDIA, POLITICS AND PUBLIC POLICY, OCTOBER 6, 2015

Kristen Soltis Anderson, co-founder of Echelon Insights, an opinion research, data analysis and digital intelligence firm, discussed the divide between the Millennial generation and the Republican Party, and what the party can do to better resonate with young voters in future elections.

While researching her book, *The Selfie Vote: Where Millennials Are Leading America* (*And How Republicans Can Keep Up*), Anderson found that the tendency of Millennials to skew liberal is not simply a function of their youth. "The way people think about politics when they first participate in the [political] process echoes throughout the rest of the decades of their lives," said Anderson. The 2008 and 2012 presidential elections were the only times a Republican candidate lost the youth vote by a margin of more than 20 percent, she said. "In order for Republicans to win a presidential election, they simply *must* do better among the Millennial generation."

Anderson said she was "cautiously optimistic" that the Republican Party could win back young voters, and even sees "a huge opportunity" for the GOP. Although young voters are "not enamored with the Republican Party," they are also disappointed in the Democratic Party, disillusioned with institutions in general, and tend to reject labels and partisanship. "This is not a generation that is fully in the tank for the Democratic Party anymore," she said.

Anderson identified three crucial areas for the GOP to focus on in order to improve its standing with Millennials.

First, Republicans need to modernize the tactics they use to reach young voters. "Republicans have lagged behind Democrats in the last few elections...in their use of social media, targeted television, the way they deploy their message," said Anderson. She identified Marco Rubio as being effective at using Snapchat to give voters a behind-the-scenes look on the campaign trail. "In a world where young voters are so distrustful of politicians, proving that politicians are real human beings...is very important."

"Just showing up in other forms of media where young people are" is also critical, said Anderson. As an example, she discussed President Obama's appearance on a web series hosted by comedian Zach Galifianakis to promote Healthcare.gov. The video became one of the most effective drivers of traffic to the website.

Next, Anderson said Republicans need to reshape their messaging to focus on "solving the problems of the future." Republican voters tend to be white, married, religious, and often own their homes and live in rural areas – all demographics that are on the decline, said Anderson. To reach young voters, the GOP needs to "make a case that they understand the new ways that Americans are living, and have policies that are adapted to that reality."

Finally, Republicans need a better understanding of Millennial values. "Becoming more libertarian" is not necessarily the answer, said Anderson. Although there are some social issues, such as gay rights, where Republicans and younger voters do diverge sharply, for other issues, such as abortion and gun control, there is less of a generational gap. Millennials are less trusting of large institutions – such as government, religion, and the media – which also has implications for economic policy. "When you say as a Republican, 'oh just trust the private sector, trust the free market,' they don't trust the free market either," said Anderson.

Championing public sector and regulatory reform to make government "more efficient, more effective and more suited to the era in which we live," presents an opportunity for the GOP. "Being a party of reforming, rather than necessarily getting rid of the government altogether, presents opportunity for a pragmatic generation."

Anderson also addressed how far-right candidates harm the image of moderate candidates, how Republicans could address climate change, the debate within the party on social issues, and differences between younger and older Millennials.

1. In the 2016 election, millennial voters were more likely to vote for Hillary Clinton than Donald Trump. Although Trump won, do you think that the author's message is still timely and will be necessary for future Republican campaigns? Why or why not?

2. Do you think that millennials are likely to change their political views as they age? Why or why not?

BIBLIOGRAPHY

Anderson, Kristen Soltis. "Kristen Soltis Anderson: Can Republicans Win Millennials in 2016?" *The Harvard Kennedy School Shorenstein Center on Media, Politics and Public,* October 6, 2015. https://shorensteincenter.org/kristen-soltis-anderson.

Aronoff, Kate. "Millennials' Non-Voting Habits, Explained." *Common Dreams,* May 08, 2016. http://www.commondreams.org/views/2016/05/08/millennials-non-voting-habits-explained.

Born, Kelly. "Millenials, Media, and Politics." *The William and Flora Hewlett Foundation,* June 5, 2015. http://www.hewlett.org/millennials-media-and-politics.

Campbell, Elizabeth, Natalie Griffin, and Amber Reece. "What You Need to Know About Millennials and Politics." *News 21,* August 24, 2016. https://cronkitenews.azpbs.org/2016/08/24/need-to-know-millennials-and-politics.

Chan, Roy Y. "Rethinking The Millennial Generation: Why Millennials Are The Future of Philanthropy, Social Justice, and the Workforce." *Philanthropy for America,* June 24, 2016. http://www.philanthropyforamerica.org/single-post/2016/06/24/Rethinking-the-Millennial-Generation-Why-Mille nnials-Are-the-Future-of-Philanthropy-Social-Justice-and -the-Workforce.

Corget, Brice, Antotonio M. Espin and Roberto Hernán-González. "Creativity and Cognitive Skills among Millennials: Thinking Too Much and Creating Too Little." *Frontiers in Psychology,* October 25, 2016. http://digitalcommons.chapman.edu/economics_articles/194.

Dutan, Frank and Carson McGrath. "How the Digital Age Changed Youth Activism." *The Ground Truth Project,* July 21, 2016. http://thegroundtruthproject.org/digital-age -millennial-activism.

Eloundou-Enyegue, Parfait. "Why Young People Aren't Keeping Up: From the Joneses to the Kardashians." *The Conversation,* June 5, 2016. https://theconversation.com/why-young-people -arent-keeping-up-from-the-joneses-to-the-kardashians-60149.

Fulton, Deirdre. "Outside RNC Headquarters, Millennials Declare: 'It's Trump vs. All of Us'." *Common Dreams,* October 6, 2016. http://www.commondreams.org/news/2016/10/06/outside -rnc-headquarters-millennials-declare-its-trump-vs-all-us.

Hoover, Eric. "The Millennial Muddle." *Chronicle of Higher Ed,* October 11, 2009. http://www.chronicle.com/article/The-Millennial-Muddle-How/48772.

Kendzior, Sarah. "The Myth of Millennial Entitlement was Created to Hide Their Parents' Mistakes." *Quartz*, June 30, 2016. http://qz.com/720456/the-myth-of-millennial -entitlement-was-created-to-hide-their-parents-mistakes.

Kotz, Paul E. "Reaching the Millennial Generation in the Classroom." *Universal Journal of Educational Research*, Volume 4, Issue 5, 2016. http://files.eric.ed.gov/fulltext/EJ1099791.pdf.

Levy, Paul. "How to Fix Work/Life Balance for Constantly Connected Millennials." *The Conversation*, July 17, 2015. http://time.com/3962801/millennial-work-life-balance.

Lewine, Gabrielle. "In Defense of Millennials." *Psychology Today*, June 8, 2016.://www.psychologytoday.com/blog/home -base/201606/in-defense-millennials.

Marcus, BK. "Millennials Reject Capitalism in Name—But Socialism in Fact." *Foundation for Economic Freedom*, May 23, 2016. https://fee.org/articles/young-people-reject-capitalism -in-name-socialism-in-fact.

McCauley, Lauren. "Report Shows Whooping $8.8 Trillion Climate Tab Being Left for Next Generation." *Common Dreams*, August 22, 2016. http://www.commondreams.org /news/2016/08/22/report-shows-whopping-88-trillion-climate -tab-being-left-next-generation.

McCoy, Nilagia. "Kristen Soltis Anderson: Can Repuvlicans Win Millennials in 2016?" *The Harvard Kennedy School Shorenstein Center on Media, Politics, and Public Policy*, October 6, 2015. https://shorensteincenter.org/kristen-soltis-anderson.

Meyer, Melissa. "How Sexting is Creating a Safe Space for Curious Millennials." *The Conversation*, March 21, 2016. https://thecon-versation.com/how-sexting-is-creating-a-safe-space-for -curious-millennials-56453.

Obama, Barack. "Why I'm Betting on You to Help Shape the New American Economy." *The White House via Medium*, October 9, 2014. https://medium.com/the-white-house/why -im-betting-on-you-to-help-shape-the-new-american -economy-e80a775b44ee#.z2fdcwudr.

Resch, Bernhard. "Labor 2.0: Why We Shouldn't Fear the 'Sharing Economy' and the Reinvention of Work." *The Conversation*, September 4, 2015. https://theconversation .com/labor-2-0-why-we-shouldnt-fear-the-sharing-economy -and-the-reinvention-of-work-46959.

Roberts, Steven and Kim Allen. "Millennials v. Baby Boomers: A Battle We Could Have Done Without." *The Conversation*,

April 6, 2016. https://theconversation.com/millennials-v-baby
-boomers-a-battle-we-could-have-done-without-57305.

Ryan, Paul. "Full Remarks: Speaker Ryan Holds Millennial Town
Hall at Georgetown." *Paul Ryan: Speaker of the House*, April 27,
2016. http://www.speaker.gov/press-release/full-remarks-
speaker-ryan-holds-millennial-town-hall-georgetown.

Slayback, Zachary. "Why Are So Few Millennials Entrepreneurs?"
Foundation for Economic Education, June 20, 2016. https://fee
.org/articles/why-are-so-few-millennials-entrepreneurs.

Stawinska, Karolina. "How Millennials Are Stepping Up To
Address UN Post 2015 Agenda Through Entrepreneurship And
Innovation." *Human Development Project*, July 7, 2015. https://
hdp.press/how-millennials-are-stepping-up-to
-address-un-post-2015-agenda-through-entrepreneurship
-and-b771f09156b9#.bve7oinx7.

Updegrove, Mark K. "Millennials: Saving the World Also Means
Running for Office." *The Catalyst*, Issue 3, Summer 2016. http://
www.bushcenter.org/catalyst/next-generation/updegrove
-saving-the-world.html.

Whibey, John. "Millennials, News and Important Trends: Research
Data from the Media Insight Project." *Journalist's Resource*,
March 19, 2015. https://journalistsresource.org/studies/society
/news-media/how-millennials-get-news-media-insight-project.

Witting, Eileen L. ""How to Leisure Like a Lazy Millennial."
The Foundation for Economic Freedom, January 5, 2017. https://
fee.org/articles/how-to-leisure-like-a-lazy-millennial.

Woo, Nicole. "Inequality, Student Debt and Millennials."
Center for Economic and Policy Research, November 12, 2014.
http://cepr.net/publications/op-eds-columns/inequality
-student-debt-and-millennials.

CHAPTER NOTES

INTRODUCTION

1. Pew Research Center, "Millennials Overtake Baby Boomers as America's Largest Generation," April 25, 2016, http://www.pewresearch.org/fact-tank/2016/04/25/millennials-overtake-baby-boomers.

2. Julia Glum, "Student Debt Crisis 2016: New Graduates Owe a Record-Breaking Average $37,000 in Loans." *International Business Times*, May 6, 2016. http://www.ibtimes.com/student-debt-crisis-2016-new-graduates-owe-record-breaking-average-37000-loans-2365195.

2. Jocelyn Kiley and Michael Dimock, "The GOP's Millennial Problem Runs Deep." *Pew Research Center*, September 25, 2014. http://www.pewresearch.org/fact-tank/2014/09/25/the-gops-millennial-problem-runs-deep.

CHAPTER 1: WHO ARE THE MILLENNIALS?

"IN DEFENSE OF MILLENNIALS" BY GABRIELLE LEWINE

Arnett, J. J. (2000). Emerging adulthood: A theory of development from the late teens through the twenties. American Psychologist, 55(5), 469-480.

De Hauw, S., & De Vos, A. (2010). Millennials' career perspective and psychological contract expectations: Does the recession lead to lowered expectations? Journal of Business and Psychology, 25(2), 293-302.

Fromm, J. (2015, November 6). Millennials in the workplace: They don't need trophies but they want reinforcement. Forbes.

Kowske, B. J., Rasch, R., & Wiley, J. (2010). Millennials' (lack of) attitude problem: An empirical examination of generational effects on work attitudes. Journal of Business and Psychology, 25(2), 265-279.

Leonard, K. (2016, January 14). Moms are older than they used to be. U.S. News & World Report.

Roisman, G. I., Masten, A. S., Coatsworth, J. D., & Tellegen, A. (2004). Salient and emerging developmental tasks in the transition to adulthood. Child Development, 75(1), 123-133.

Rosato, D. (2015, May 18). Millennials want work-life balance too. Here's how they can get it. Time.

Safer, M. (Correspondent). (2007, November 11). The "millennials" are coming [Television series episode]. In 60 Minutes. CBS.

Stein, J. (2013, May 20). Millennials: The me me me generation. Time.

Thompson, C., & Gregory, J. B. (2012). Managing millennials: A framework for improving attraction, motivation, and retention. The Psychologist-Manager Journal, 15(4), 237-246.

Twaronite, K. (2015). Study: Work-life challenges across generations: Millennials and parents hit hardest. Retrieved from http://www.ey.com/US/en/About-us/Our-people-and-culture/EY-work-life-cha...

White, G. B. (2015, November 30). Do millennials make for bad employees? The Atlantic.

CHAPTER 3: MILLENNIALS AND ACTIVISM

"RETHINKING THE MILLENNIAL GENERATION: WHY MILLENNIALS ARE THE FUTURE OF PHILANTHROPY, SOCIAL JUSTICE, AND THE WORKFORCE" BY ROY Y. CHAN

Blackbaud (2013). *The next generation of American giving: The charitable habits of generation Y, X, baby boomers, and matures.* Charleston, SC: Blackbaud.

Bremmer, R. H. (1988). *American philanthropy.* Chicago, IL: The University of Chicago Press.
Case Foundation (2015). *2015 millennial impactful report: Causes, influences, and the next generation workforce.* Washington, D.C.: Achieve and The Case Foundation.

Gallup (2016). *How millennials want to work and live.* Washington, D.C.: Gallup.

Giving USA Foundation (2016). *Giving USA 2016: The annual report on philanthropy for the year 2015.* Chicago, IL.

Goodman, L. M. (2015, June). "Millennial college graduates: Young, educated, jobless." *Newsweek.* Retrieved from http://www.newsweek.com/2015/06/05/millennial-college-graduates-young-educated-jobless-335821.html

Kuhl, J. (2014). *The college student mindset: For career preparation and success.* New York, NY: Why Millennial Matters.

Pew Research Center (2016, April). "Millennials overtake Baby Boomers as America's largest generation." Retrieved from: http://www.pewresearch.org/fact-tank/2016/04/25/millennials-overtake-baby-boomers/

ProInspire (2015). "A force of impact: Millennials in the nonprofit sector." Retrieved from http://www.proinspire.org/wp-content/uploads/2015/10/ProInspire-Millennials-in-the-Nonprofit-Sector-report-2015-digital.pdf

U.S. Census Bureau (2016). "2016 Population Estimates." Retrieved from http://www.census.gov/popest/data/datasets.html?eml=gd&utm_medium=email&utm_source=govdelivery

CHAPTER 5: RESEARCH ON MILLENNIALS

"CREATIVITY AND COGNITIVE SKILLS AMONG MILLENNIALS: THINKING TOO MUCH AND CREATING TOO LITTLE" BY BRICE CORGNET, ANTONIO M. ESPIN, AND ROBERTO HERNÁN-GONZÁLEZ

1. See the following press release: http://www.forbes.com/sites/susanadams/2012/09/24/older-workers-theres-hope-study

-finds-employers-like-you-better-than-millennials/#1f5799c-
b4aa6 (accessed September 21, 2016).
2. Positive effects of cognitive reflection on people's willingness
   to choose socially-efficient resource allocations (Lohse, 2016;
   Capraro et al., 2016) as well as to trust strangers (Corgnet et al.,
   2016) suggest other possible channels through which organizations may benefit from hiring individuals with a more reflective cognitive style. Cognitive reflection has also been found
   to play a key role in moral judgment (e.g., Paxton et al., 2012;
   Pennycook et al. 2014).

REFERENCES

Abraham, A. (2014). Is there an inverted-U relationship between
   creativity and psychopathology? *Front. Psychol.* 5:750. doi:
   10.3389/fpsyg.2014.00750
Abraham, A., Windmann, S., McKenna, P., and Güntürkün, O.
   (2007). Creative thinking in schizophrenia: the role of executive
   dysfunction and symptom severity. *Cogn. Neuropsychiatry* 12,
   235–258. doi: 10.1080/135468006010 46714
Acar, S., and Sen, S. (2013). A multilevel meta-analysis of the relationship between creativity and schizotypy. *Psychol. Aesthetics
   Creativity Arts* 7:214. doi: 10.1037/a0031975
Allen, A. P., and Thomas, K. E. (2011). A dual process account
   of creative thinking. *Creativity Res. J.* 23, 109–118. doi:
   10.1080/10400419.2011.571183
Ball, L. J., Marsh, J. E., Litchfield, D., Cook, R. L., and Booth,
   N. (2015). When distraction helps: evidence that con-
   current articulation and irrelevant speech can facilitate
   insight problem solving. *Thinking Reasoning* 21, 76–96. doi:
   10.1080/13546783.2014.934399
Barr, N., Pennycook, G., Stolz, J. A., and Fugelsang, J. A.
   (2015). Reasoned connections: a dual-process perspective on creative thought. *Thinking Reasoning* 21, 61–75. doi:
   10.1080/13546783.2014.895915
Basadur, M. S. (1995). Optimal ideation-evaluation ratios.
   Creativity Res. J. 8, 63–75. doi: 10.1207/s15326934crj0801_5
Batey, M., and Furnham, A. (2006). Creativity, intelligence, and
   personality. *Genet. Soc. Gen. Psychol. Monogr.* 132, 355–429. doi:
   10.3200/MONO.132.4.355-430
Beaty, R. E., and Silvia, P. J. (2012). Why do ideas get more creative
   across time? An executive interpretation of the serial order

effect in divergent thinking tasks. *Psychol. Aesthetics Creativity Arts* 6:309. doi: 10.1037/a0029171

Bosch-Domènech, A., Brañas-Garza, P., and Espín, A. M. (2014). Can exposure to prenatal sex hormones (2D: 4D) predict cognitive reflection? *Psychoneuroendocrinology* 43, 1–10. doi: 10.1016/j.psyneuen.2014.01.023

Brañas-Garza, P., García-Muñoz, T., and Hernán-González, R. (2012). Cognitive effort in the beauty contest game. *J. Econ. Behav. Organ.* 83, 254–260. doi: 10.1016/j.jebo.2012.05.018

Capraro, V., Corgnet, B., Espín, A. M., and Hernán-González, R. (2016). Deliberation favors social efficiency by helping people disregard their relative shares: evidence from US and India. Available online at: SSRN: http://ssrn.com/abstract=2799850

Chermahini, S. A., and Hommel, B. (2010). The (b) link between creativity and dopamine: spontaneous eye blink rates predict and dissociate divergent and convergent thinking. *Cognition* 115, 458–465. doi: 10.1016/j.cognition. 2010.03.007

Cleveland, W. S. (1979). Robust locally weighted regression and smoothing scatterplots. *J. Am. Stat. Assoc.* 74, 829–836. doi: 10.1080/01621459.1979. 10481038

Cleveland, W. S., and McGill, R. (1985). Graphical perception and graphical methods for analyzing scientific data. *Science* 229, 828–833. doi: 10.1126/ science.229.4716.828

Cohen, J. D., and Servan-Schreiber, D. (1992). Context, cortex, and dopamine: a connectionist approach to behavior and biology in schizophrenia. *Psychol. Rev.* 99, 45–77.

Cokely, E. T., and Kelley, C. M. (2009). Cognitive abilities and superior decision making under risk: a protocol analysis and process model evaluation. *Judgment Decision Making* 4:20.

Corgnet, B., Espín, A. M., and Hernán-González, R. (2015a). The cognitive basis of social behavior: cognitive reflection overrides antisocial but not always prosocial motives. *Front. Behav. Neurosci.* 9:287. doi: 10.3389/fnbeh.2015. 00287

Corgnet, B., Espín, A. M., Hernán-González, R., Kujal, P., and Rassenti, S. (2016). To trust, or not to trust: cognitive reflection in trust games. *J. Behav. Exp. Econ.* 64, 20–27. doi: 10.1016/j. socec.2015.09.008

Corgnet, B., Hernán-González, R., and Mateo, R. (2015b). Cognitive reflection and the diligent worker: an experimental study

of millennials. *PloS ONE* 10:e0141243. doi: 10.1371/journal.
pone.0141243

Dilchert, S., Ones, D. S., Davis, R. D., and Rostow, C. D. (2007).
Cognitive ability predicts objectively measured counterproductive work behaviors. *J. Appl. Psychol.* 92:616. doi: 10.1037/
0021-9010.92.3.616

Dorfman, J., Shames, V. A., and Kihlstrom, J. F. (1996). "Intuition,
incubation, and insight: implicit cognition in problem solving,"
in *Implicit Cognition*, ed G. Underwood (Oxford: Oxford
University Press), 257–296.

Evans, J. S. B. T. (2008). Dual-processing accounts of reasoning,
judgment, and social cognition. *Annu. Rev. Psychol.* 59, 255–278.
doi: 10.1146/annurev.psych.59.103006.093629

Evans, J. S. B. T. (2009). "How many dual-process theories do we
need? One, two, or many?" in *In Two Minds: Dual Processes and
Beyond*, eds Evans, J. S. B. T. and K. Frankish (New York, NY:
Oxford University Press), 33–55.

Evans, J. S. B. T., and Stanovich, K. E. (2013). Dual-process theo-
ries of higher cognition advancing the debate. *Perspect. Psychol.
Sci.* 8, 223–241. doi: 10.1177/1745691612460685 Eysenck, H.
J. (1993). Creativity and personality: suggestions for a theory.
Psychol. Inquiry 4, 147–178. doi: 10.1207/s15327965pli0403_1

Finke, R. A., Ward, T. B., and Smith, S. M. (1992). Creative
Cognition: Theory, Research and Applications. Cambridge, MA:
MIT Press.

Frederick, S. (2005). Cognitive reflection and decision making. *J.
Econ. Perspect.* 19, 25–42. doi: 10.1257/089533005775196732

Gabora, L. (2005). Creative thought as a non-Darwinian evolution-
ary process. *J. Creat. Behav.* 39, 262–283. doi: 10.1002/j.2162-
6057.2005.tb01261.x

Gabora, L., and Ranjan, A. (2013). "How insight emerges in dis-
tributed, contentaddressable memory," in *The Neuroscience of
Creativity*, eds A. Bristol, O. Vartanian, and J. Kaufman (New
York, NY: Oxford University Press), 19–44.

Getzels, J. W., and Jackson, P. W. (1962). *Creativity and Intelligence:
Explorations with Gifted Students.* New York, NY: Wiley.

Gilhooly, K. J., Fioratou, E., Anthony, S. H., and Wynn, V. (2007).
Divergent thinking: strategies and executive involvement in
generating novel uses for familiar objects. *Br. J. Psychol.* 98,
611–625. doi: 10.1111/j.2044- 8295.2007.tb00467.x

Guilford, J. P. (1967). *The Nature of Human Intelligence.* New York, NY: McGrawHill. Hocevar, D. (1979). Ideational fluency as a confounding factor in the measurement of originality. *J. Educ. Psychol.* 71:191. doi: 10.1037/0022-0663.71.2.191

Howard-Jones, P. A. (2002). A dual-state model of creative cognition for supporting strategies that foster creativity in the classroom. *Int. J. Technol. Design Educ.* 12, 215–226. doi: 10.1023/A:1020243429353

Hunter, J. E., and Hunter, R. F. (1984). Validity and utility of alternative predictors of job performance. *Psychol. Bull.* 96, 72–98. doi: 10.1037/0033-2909.96.1.72

Jaeggi, S. M., Studer-Luethi, B., Buschkuehl, M., Su, Y. F., Jonides, J., and Perrig, W. J. (2010). The relationship between n-back performance and matrix reasoning – implications for training and transfer. *Intelligence* 38, 625–635. doi: 10.1016/j.intell.2010.09.001

Jaracz, J., Patrzala, A., and Rybakowski, J. K. (2012). Creative thinking deficits in patients with schizophrenia: neurocognitive correlates. *J. Nerv. Ment. Dis.* 200, 588–593. doi: 10.1097/NMD.0b013e31825bfc49

Jarosz, A. F., Colflesh, G. J. H., and Wiley, J. (2012). Uncorking the muse: alcohol intoxication facilitates creative problem solving. *Conscious. Cogn.* 21, 487–493. doi: 10.1016/j.concog.2012.01.002

Jauk, E., Benedek, M., Dunst, B., and Neubauer, A. C. (2013). The relationship between intelligence and creativity: new support for the threshold hypothesis by means of empirical breakpoint detection. *Intelligence* 41, 212–221. doi: 10.1016/j.intell.2013.03.003

Kahneman, D., and Frederick, S. (2007). Frames and brains: elicitation and control of response tendencies. *Trends Cogn. Sci.* 11, 45–46. doi: 10.1016/j.tics.2006.11.007

Karson, C. N. (1983). Spontaneous eye-blink rates and dopaminergic systems. *Brain* 106, 643–653.

Kaufman, J. C. (2009). *Creativity 101.* New York, NY: Springer Publishing Company.

Kim, K. H. (2005). Can only intelligent people be creative? A meta-analysis. *J. Secondary Gifted Educ.* 16, 57–66. doi: 10.4219/jsge-2005-473

Kim, K. H., Cramond, B., and VanTassel-Baska, J. (2010). "The relationship between creativity and intelligence," in *The*

Cambridge Handbook of Creativity, eds J. C. Kaufman and R. J. Sternberg (New York, NY: Cambridge University Press), 395–412.

Kim, S., Hasher, L., and Zacks, R. T. (2007). Aging and a benefit of distractibility. *Psychonomic Bull. Rev. 14*, 301–305. doi: 10.3758/BF031 94068

Kovacevic, S., Azma, S., Irimia, A., Sherfey, J., Halgren, E., and Marinkovic, K. (2012). Theta oscillations are sensitive to both early and late conflict processing stages: effects of alcohol intoxication. *PloS ONE* 7:e43957. doi: 10.1371/journal.pone.0043957

Lohse, J. (2016). Smart or selfish–when smart guys finish nice. *J. Behav. Exp. Econ.* 64, 28–40. doi: 10.1016/j.socec.2016.04.002

Marinkovic, K., Rickenbacher, E., Azma, S., and Artsy, E. (2012). Acute alcohol intoxication impairs top–down regulation of stroop incongruity as revealed by blood oxygen level? dependent functional magnetic resonance imaging. *Human Brain Map.* 33, 319–333. doi: 10.1002/hbm. 21213

Mednick, S. A. (1962). The associative basis of the creative process. *Psychol. Rev.* 69, 220. doi: 10.1037/h0048850

Murphy, K. R. (1989). Is the relationship between cognitive ability and job performance stable over time? *Human Perform.* 2, 183–200. doi: 10.1207/s15327043hup0203_3

Nijstad, B. A., De Dreu, C. K. W., Rietzschel, E. F., and Baas, M. (2010). The dual pathway to creativity model: creative ideation as a function of flexibility and persistence. *Eur. Rev. Soc. Psychol.* 21, 34–77. doi: 10.1080/10463281003765323

Norris, P., and Epstein, S. (2011). An experiential thinking style: its facets and relations with objective and subjective criterion measures. *J. Personal.* 79, 1043–1080. doi: 10.1111/j.1467-6494.2011.00718.x

Nusbaum, E. C., and Silvia, P. J. (2011). Are intelligence and creativity really so different? Fluid intelligence, executive processes, and strategy use in divergent thinking. *Intelligence* 39, 36–45. doi: 10.1016/j.intell.2010.11.002

Oechssler, J., Roider, A., and Schmitz, P. W. (2009). Cognitive abilities and behavioral biases. *J. Econ. Behav. Organ.* 72, 147–152. doi: 10.1016/j.jebo.2009.04.018

Olea, M. M., and Ree, M. J. (1994). Predicting pilot and navigator criteria: not much more than g. *J. Appl. Psychol.* 79, 845–851. doi: 10.1037/0021-9010.79.6.845

Paxton, J. M., Unger, L., and Greene, J. D. (2012). Reflection and reasoning in moral judgement. *Cogn. Sci.* 36, 163–177. doi: 10.1111/j.1551-6709.2011.01210.x

Pennycook, G., Cheyne, J. A., Barr, N., Koehler, D. J., and Fugelsang, J. A. (2014). The role of analytic thinking in moral judgements and values. *Thinking Reasoning* 20, 188–214. doi: 10.1080/13546783.2013.865000

Peterson, J. B., Rothfleisch, J., Zelazo, P. D., and Pihl, R. O. (1990). Acute alcohol intoxication and cognitive functioning. *J. Stud. Alcohol* 51, 114–122. doi: 10.15288/jsa.1990.51.114

Pink, D. (2005). *A Whole New Mind.* New York City, NY: Riverhead Books.

Rainer, T. S., and Rainer, J. W. (2011). *The Millennials: Connecting to America's Largest Generation.* Nashville, TN: B and H Publishing Group.

Raven, J. C. (1936). *Mental Tests used in Genetic Studies: The Performances of Related Individuals in Tests Mainly Educative and Mainly Reproductive.* Unpublished master's thesis, University of London.

Ricks, T. R., Turley-Ames, K. J., and Wiley, J. (2007). Effects of working memory capacity on mental set due to domain knowledge. *Mem. Cogn.* 35, 1456–1462. doi: 10.3758/BF03193615

Runco, M. A. (2007). *Creativity.* San Diego, CA: Acade.

Sawyer, R. K. (2006). *Explaining Creativity: The Science of Human Innovation.* New York, NY: Oxford University Press.

Schmidt, F. L. (2009). "Select on intelligence," in *Handbook of Principles of Organizational Behavior: Indispensable Knowledge for Evidence-Based Management*, ed E. A. Locke (New York, NY: John Wiley and Sons, Ltd.), 3–18.

Schmidt, F. L., Hunter, J. E., and Outerbridge, A. N. (1986). Impact of job experience and ability on job knowledge, work sample performance, and supervisory ratings of job performance. *J. Appl. Psychol.* 71:432. doi: 10.1037/0021-9010.71.3.432

Schuldberg, D. (2005). Eysenck Personality Questionnaire scales and paper-and-pencil tests related to creativity. *Psychol. Rep.* 97, 180–182. doi: 10.2466/pr0.97.5.180-182

Silvia, P. J. (2008a). Another look at creativity and intelligence: exploring higher-order models and probable confounds. *Pers. Individ. Diff.* 44, 1012–1021. doi: 10.1016/j.paid.2007.10.027

Silvia, P. J. (2008b). Creativity and intelligence revisited: a latent variable analysis of Wallach and Kogan (1965). *Creativity Res. J.*

20, 34–39. doi: 10.1080/10400410701841807

Silvia, P. J. (2015). Intelligence and creativity are pretty similar after all. *Educ. Psychol. Rev.* 27, 599–606. doi: 10.1007/s10648-015-9299-1

Silvia, P. J., Winterstein, B. P., Willse, J. T., Barona, C. M., Cram, J. T., Hess, K. I., et al. (2008). Assessing creativity with divergent thinking tasks: exploring the reliability and validity of new subjective scoring methods. *Psychol. Aesthetics Creativity Arts* 2, 68–85. doi: 10.1037/1931-3896.2.2.68

Sowden, P. T., Pringle, A., and Gabora, L. (2015). The shifting sands of creative thinking: connections to dual-process theory. *Thinking Reasoning* 21, 40–60. doi: 10.1080/13546783.2014.885464

Stanovich, K. E. (2009). "Distinguishing the reflective, algorithmic, and autonomous minds: is it time for a tri-process theory," in *In Two Minds: Dual Processes and Beyond*, eds J. S. B. T. Evans and K. Frankish (New York, NY: Oxford University Press), 55–88.

Stanovich, K. E. (2010). *Rationality and the Reflective Mind.* Oxford University Press.

Toplak, M. E., West, R. F., and Stanovich, K. E. (2011). The cognitive reflection test as a predictor of performance on heuristics and biases tasks. *Mem. Cogn.* 39, 1275–1289. doi: 10.3758/s13421-011-0104-1

Toplak, M. E., West, R. F., and Stanovich, K. E. (2014). Assessing miserly information processing: an expansion of the cognitive reflection test. *Thinking Reasoning* 20, 147–168. doi: 10.1080/13546783.2013.844729

Troyer, A. K., and Moscovitch, M. (2006). "Cognitive processes of verbal fluency tasks," in *The Quantified Process Approach to Neuropsychological Assessment*, ed A. M. Poreh (New York, NY: Taylor and Francis Group), 143–157.

Wallach, M. A., and Kogan, N. (1965). *Modes of Thinking in Young Children: A Study of the Creativity-Intelligence Distinction*. New York, NY: Holt, Rinehart and Winston.

Weisberg, R. W. (2006). *Creativity: Understanding Innovation in Problem Solving, Science, Invention, and the Arts.* Hoboken, NJ: John Wiley and Sons.

Wiley, J., and Jarosz, A. F. (2012a). "How working memory capacity affects problem solving," in *Psychology of Learning and Motivation*, Vol. 56, ed B. H. Ross (Burlington, MA: Academic Press), 185–228.

Wiley, J., and Jarosz, A. F. (2012b). Working memory capacity, attentional focus, and problem solving. *Curr. Direct. Psychol. Sci.* 21, 258–262 doi: 10.1177/0963721412447622

"REACHING THE MILLENNIAL GENERATION IN THE CLASSROOM" BY PAUL E. KOTZ

[1] Allen, Christopher (2012). *Generational Teaching: Motivating the Minority*, 1st ed. Retrieved June 1st, 2013, from http://books.google.com/books?id=77HNPGzfVSUC&pg

[2] Elliot-Yeary, Sherri. (2012). Generation Y- The Millennial Generation. *Generational Guru*. Retrieved May 25, 2013, from http://generationalguru.com/2012/02/generation-ythe-millennial-generation.

[3] Gallagher, R. (2008). National Survey of Counseling Center Directors. The International Association of Counseling Centers, Inc. Retrieved January 10, 2009 from http://www.iacsinc.org.

[4] Lynch, Art. (2013). *Generation Me! The Millennial Generation*. Retrieved May 28, 2013 from http://www.comprofessor.com/2009/12/millenial-generationers-are-changing.html

[5] Manning, Terry M (2013). Who are the Millennials? *Central Piedmont Community College*. Retrieved May 24, 2013, from https://www.cpcc.edu/millennial.

[6] Wilson, Michael, & Gerber E. Leslie. (2008). How Generational Theory Can Improve Teaching: Strategies for Working with the "Millennials" [Electronic Version]. *Currents In Teaching And Learning*, 1, 29-39.

GLOSSARY

altruism—Doing things for the benefit of others and without self-serving intentions.

archetype—One thing or person that represents a universal trend or pattern.

Baby Boomers—Those who were born between 1946 and 1964. Baby Boomers are the only generation with specifically defined bracket years.

conservatism—Political philosophies that are traditional and do not support broad change in social and cultural areas.

digital natives—People who grew up with digital technology, like smartphones or the internet.

disillusioned—To have lost faith or belief in something that was once valued as good and positive.

draconian—Anything that is harsh, strict, or outdated.

entrepreneurship—To start a business or other venture.

gaslighting—Manipulating someone through psychological means into questioning their own sanity.

Generation X—Those who were born between the late 1960s and the early 1980s.

gig economy—Refers to the rise of casual or temporary work, often completed without contracts by independent workers.

Great Recession—A period of economic trouble that took place in the late 2000s, when the economy suffered its worst downturn since the Great Depression. It resulted in numerous job losses, business closures, and long lasting effects on the workforce.

individualistic—To be focused on the individual or considered unconventional. Millennials are often considered individualistic because they are seen as breaking with tradition and are independent.

pigeonhole—To confine a group to a small and overly simplified definition.

pragmatist—Someone who takes a practical approach to a problem without letting emotion influence or distract them.

progressive—Philosophies and ideologies that support social change and liberal policies.

stereotype—A commonly held idea that is untrue, too general, or otherwise lacking in depth.

turmoil—Chaos, uncertainty, or disorder.

upward mobility—The ability of individuals to reach a higher social or economic level than they were previously at, such as a lower-income worker reaching the economic middle class.

FOR MORE INFORMATION

BOOKS

Anderson, Kristen Soltis. *The Selfie Vote: Where Millennials Are Leading America (And How Republicans Can Keep Up)*. New York, NY: HarperCollins, 2015.

Bryson, Sam B. *In Defense of the Peter Pan Generation*. Amazon Digital, 2016.

Burstein, David D. *Fast Future: How the Millennial Generation is Shaping our World*. Boston, MA: Beacon Press, 2013.

Cahn, David and Jack Cahn. *When Millennials Rule: The Reshaping of America*. New York, NY: Post Hill Press, 2016.

Carson, Elan M. *The Millennial Mentality: More Than Memes, Cats & Mishaps.* Elan Carson, 2015.

Keegan, Marina. *The Opposite of Loneliness: Essays and Stories*. New York, NY: Scribner, 2014.

Luttrell, Regina and Karen McGrath. *The Millennial Mindset: Unraveling Fact from Fiction*. Lanham, MA: Rowman & Littlefield, 2015.

Price, Michael. *What's Next? The Millennial's Guide to Surviving and Thriving in the Real World*. Delray Beach, FL: Priceless Media Group, 2013.

Rosenstein, Andrew. *A Millennial World: Understanding the Drive of a Rising Generation*. Austin, TX: Lioncrest, 2016.

Taylor, Paul. *The Next America: Boomers, Millennials, and the Looming Generational Showdown*. New York, NY: PublicAffairs, 2016.

WEBSITES

Mic

www.mic.com

Founded in 2011 by Chris Altchek and Jake Horowitz, this news
site covers current events and entertainment from a millennial
perspective and is based on the belief that "millennials are
inquisitive, have a healthy skepticism for conventional wisdom,
and crave substantive news to spark interesting conversations."

The Millennial Impact

www.themillienialimpact.com

This organization researches and releases reports on millennials, causes they support, and how they engage with the world
around them.

Pew Research Center

www.pewresearch.org

The Pew Research Center is a nonpartisan research think tank
that offers comprehensive studies on millennials, how they
compare to other generations, and issues they care about,
among other issues.

INDEX

ABOUT THE EDITOR

Bridey Heing is a writer and book critic based in Washington, DC. She holds degrees in political science and international affairs from DePaul University and Washington University in Saint Louis. Her areas of focus are comparative politics and Iranian politics. Her master's thesis explores the evolution of populist politics and democracy in Iran since 1900. She has written about Iranian affairs, women's rights, and art and politics for publications like the *Economist*, *Hyperallergic*, and the *Establishment*. She also writes about literature and film. She enjoys traveling, reading, and exploring Washington, DC's many museums.